Teaching *Character*
IN THE PRIMARY CLASSROOM

SAGE was founded in 1965 by Sara Miller McCune to support the dissemination of usable knowledge by publishing innovative and high-quality research and teaching content. Today, we publish over 900 journals, including those of more than 400 learned societies, more than 800 new books per year, and a growing range of library products including archives, data, case studies, reports, and video. SAGE remains majority-owned by our founder, and after Sara's lifetime will become owned by a charitable trust that secures our continued independence.

Los Angeles | London | New Delhi | Singapore | Washington DC | Melbourne

Teaching *Character*

IN THE PRIMARY CLASSROOM

TOM **HARRISON** | IAN **MORRIS** | JOHN **RYAN**

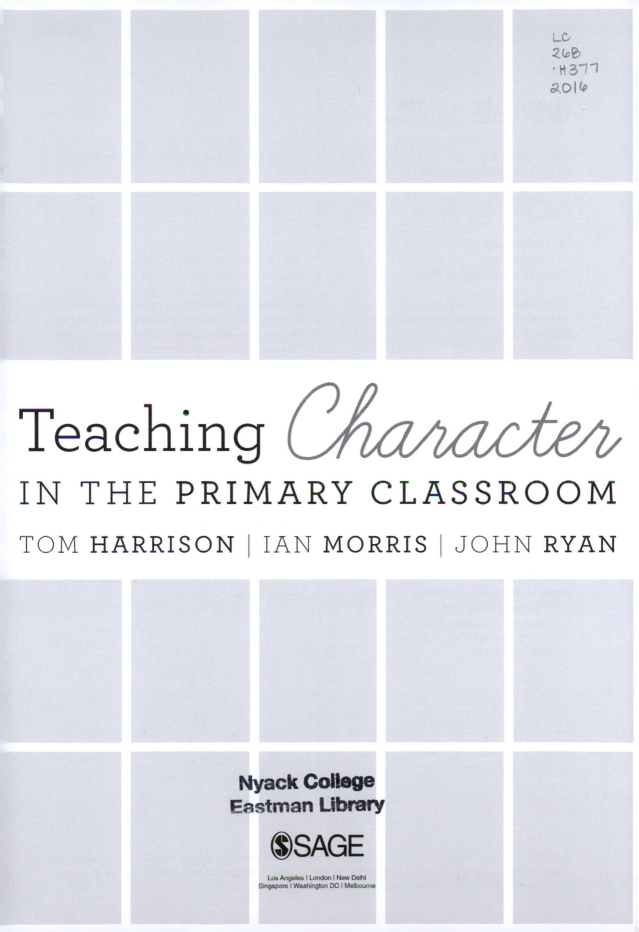

⑤SAGE

Los Angeles | London | New Delhi
Singapore | Washington DC | Melbourne

Learning Matters
An imprint of SAGE Publications Ltd
1 Oliver's Yard
55 City Road
London EC1Y 1SP

SAGE Publications Inc.
2455 Teller Road
Thousand Oaks, California 91320

SAGE Publications India Pvt Ltd
B 1/I 1 Mohan Cooperative Industrial Area
Mathura Road
New Delhi 110 044

SAGE Publications Asia-Pacific Pte Ltd
3 Church Street
#10–04 Samsung Hub
Singapore 049483

Editor: Kate Wharton
Production Controller: Chris Marke
Project Management: Deer Park Productions,
    Tavistock, Devon
Marketing Manager: Lorna Patkai
Cover Design: Wendy Scott
Typeset by: C&M Digitals (P) Ltd, Chennai, India
Printed and bound by CPI Group (UK) Ltd,
    Croydon, CR0 4YY

Library of Congress Control Number: 2015959703

British Library Cataloguing in Publication Data

A catalogue record for this book is available from the British Library.

ISBN: 978-1-4739-5217-1
ISBN: 978-1-4739-5216-4 (hbk)

At SAGE we take sustainability seriously. Most of our products are printed in the UK using FSC papers and boards. When we print overseas we ensure sustainable papers are used as measured by the PREPS grading system. We undertake an annual audit to monitor our sustainability.

Contents

About the authors

Tom Harrison

Tom Harrison is Director of Education at the Jubilee Centre for Character and Virtues in the University of Birmingham. At the Centre he takes a leading role on several research and development projects and in particular those relating to character education. He has extensive experience of designing, developing and delivering character education programmes as well as teaching about the subject.

Ian Morris

Ian Morris is Head of Well-being at Wellington College in Berkshire. He has taught religious studies and well-being in the independent and state sectors since 2000. Ian has written a guide to teaching well-being in schools and has led training and professional development for teachers in well-being and character education in the UK and abroad.

John Ryan

John Ryan is Director of Primary Education at the University of Birmingham. At the University of Birmingham he is responsible for the PGCE Dip Ed course and he teaches professional studies. Previously John worked as a senior lecturer at Newman University and he has worked in many primary schools in the West Midlands.

Preface

The role schools and teachers play in building the character of their pupils has been coming under increasing scrutiny. As such, character education is currently experiencing a resurgence of interest amongst educational policy makers, researchers, teachers, employers, parents, children and young people. However, those on the front line of delivering character education in primary schools report being unfamiliar with the increasing amount of empirical research and practical advice on the theme. As a consequence of such unfamiliarity, the notion of character education could have the potential to become inconsistent, meaningless and tokenistic, even damaging, if not handled and taught sensitively. This book aims to fill this void, by providing clear, accessible advice on how teachers and other educators can successfully enhance character education provision in their schools. Core themes are covered, such as: what is, and what is not character education; why character matters; the roles and responsibilities of teachers as character educators; and measuring character. The book features practical advice throughout, including lesson ideas and resources for taught and caught approaches to character education. The aim of the book is not only to make the case for character education and inspire teachers, but also to provide the practical tools and advice that primary school teachers interested in the subject can adopt and implement.

Part 1

Introducing character education

Part 1 of this book provides a background to character education. Chapter 1 makes the case for why character matters as well as outlining why character education is seeing a resurgence in the UK and elsewhere. Chapter 2 describes what character and character education are, and, just as importantly, what character education is not. In this chapter a description of the different types of virtues that make up character are described – these are often considered the building blocks of character. Chapter 3 covers the theory behind character education and describes how different disciplines conceive of the subject. This includes a discussion on Aristotelian virtue ethics which is viewed by many as the best philosophical basis for the subject. Recent trends in psychology and positive education and well-being are also explored and there is also a section on the trials and tribulations of measuring character. Chapter 4, the final chapter in the section, deals with the 'can character be taught?' debate. It shows that character education might be best considered as more than 'just a subject' as it is both caught and taught. Parts 2 and 3 provide examples of how the 'taught' and 'caught' approaches to character education can be applied in practice.

1 Character matters

In this chapter you will:

- read about why character matters;
- be introduced to character education;
- read a brief history of character education in the UK;
- be provided with an overview of the book.

Character matters: The elephant in the interview room. . .

Imagine this scenario...

You are on your way to achieving Qualified Teacher Status and you have managed to get an interview for your first teaching job in a primary school near where you live. You have done well in your training, your grades are good and you feel confident as you prepare for the interview. In the interview you demonstrate your knowledge of a range of topics including inclusion, safeguarding, attainment, behaviour, subject knowledge and progress – amongst others. You teach a good demonstration lesson. You feel quietly confident as you leave the interview...

You don't get the job...

You reconcile yourself with the thought that there were several other good candidates going for the job. But your mind won't let it go and you keep wondering what you did wrong in the interview. The answer might be you did nothing wrong, but the interviewers (fairly or unfairly) made a judgement about your character and decided that the character of one of the other candidates aligned more closely with the mission, aims, ethos and culture of their school.

The spoken (or often unspoken) reflections of the interviewers after you left the room are likely to have been questions such as: would you *fit* in the school?; what would you be like to be managed?; are you a team player?; are you likely to be resilient and adaptable when the going gets tough?; will you be supportive and caring towards the pupils?; what type of role model will you be for the pupils? These are the unspoken questions of character that are part and parcel of most interviews. Often this is with good reason, for as the Jubilee Centre's statement on teacher education and character education states (Jubilee Centre, 2015) *'the single most powerful tool a teacher has to impact on a student's character is their own character'*. After all, whether stated or not, good teachers are not those who can simply deliver good content but those who model good character in practice. As David Carr (2007) notes, *'It is often said that we remember teachers as much for the kinds of people they were than for anything they may have taught us, and some kinds of professional expertise may best be understood as qualities of character'* (p.369).

Judgements of character are almost always the elephant in the interview room.

Of course, judgements of character are often subjective. This is why schools and other employers have increasingly more sophisticated interview programmes involving a series of activities designed to tease out a candidate's character and values and how they interact in group settings. However, in a traditional face-to-face interview you might be able to demonstrate you have the qualification, skills and knowledge for the job: but can you convince the panel you have the character?

Character matters in all of the myriad roles we play in our lives. Not just as a prospective employee trying to get a job, but also when we are actually doing the job. Likewise character matters in the many roles we play outside of work – as parents, relatives, neighbours and friends. Ultimately it is our character that determines how successfully we carry out these roles: whether we are compassionate to our neighbours, honest with our friends, courageous in our work or responsible in our parenting. Just as often we notice when people don't display these qualities of moral character as when they do. A quick trawl through almost any newspaper demonstrates this. Consider the list below of some of the bigger scandals that have taken place over the last few years:

- The banking crisis, where millions of pounds was lost through bankers bending and sometimes breaking the law.

- The Mid Staffordshire NHS Foundation Trust scandal, where the care and compassion of some of the nurses at Stafford Hospital was called into question.

- The Hillsborough tragedy, which exposed a police cover-up.

- Some MPs over-claiming on expenses.

- Some journalists at some newspapers hacking into private voicemails.

All these stories have questions of character at their heart. At some level in each of these stories, we see character flaws, or vices, being played out. They often provoke outrage in us, as the protagonists, either through negligence or bad will, are caught up in events which result in damage, loss or harm. We, in turn, are caught up in moral judgements about what has happened. Questions of character are inextricably bound up in the business of daily human life.

On the flip side, let's consider what makes a 'good' news story: athletes showing determination and grit to win an Olympic gold medal; the courageous acts of whistleblowers who expose wrongdoing in our public and private institutions; the public figure who does a good deed for charity, campaigns on an important issue or who gives away their money to good causes; the local hero who has made a difference to their community or the emergency worker who has shown bravery in a dangerous situation. Our fascination with and desire to celebrate stories such as these demonstrate to us the enduring appeal of outstanding character.

It is clear as we read the news that we understand what is right or wrong, good or bad. We understand from our own experiences that the virtues we display determine the outcome of our own personal stories and that therefore, character matters. If character matters to us as adults, this clearly implies the importance of the development of the character of young people and helps to explain why, as we will see below, character education is being taken increasingly seriously by both policy makers and teachers.

Not just another fad: a brief history of character education

Character education is not just another educational fad – and it certainly is not new. Good education from the beginning of time has included character education. It might not be called 'character education' and teachers might not even be aware they are developing character, but few primary school teachers would claim that they didn't hope to have a positive influence on the character of their pupils. After all, many teachers go into the profession wanting to make a difference and to positively transform the lives of young people. It might be argued that every day in every school, every teacher is educating their pupils in character. The key question is, are they doing it well or badly?

In order to explain the recent resurgence in interest in character education, it is helpful to understand the recent history of the subject. Although it may not always have been referred to as character education, there has been a long history of policy intentions – either explicitly or implicitly expressed – to develop the character in pupils in schools in the UK. In his book *Education with Character*, James Arthur provides an excellent overview of the history of character education. In it he states that:

> *The formation of character could be said to be the aim that all general education has historically set out to achieve. It is an aim that has often not been explicitly stated: it has simply been assumed.*
>
> (Arthur, 2003, p.11)

Arthur's book charts character education back to the philosophy of Plato and Aristotle. It also acknowledges the influence of Robert Owen and the Institute for the Formation of Character that he established in 1816. It charts character education through the Victorian era up to the present day and, in particular, recent government policy.

The recent interest in character education in the UK perhaps starts with the 1988 Education Reform Act, which established a framework for the development of the national curriculum, underpinned by two core aims: to promote the spiritual, moral, cultural, mental and physical development of pupils; and to prepare pupils for the opportunities, responsibilities and experiences of adult life (Children Schools and Families Committee, 2009). Although character is not mentioned in these overarching aims, it is clear that they are both about the development of different types of character qualities with the intention they will prepare young people for their future roles in life. When the Labour government came to power in 1997 their first White Paper on education, *Excellence in Schools*, laid out the need for pupils to '*develop the strength of character and attitudes to life and work*'. At around the same time, the subject of citizenship education was also being established. The new subject was very much about developing character in young people to prepare them to be responsible and active citizens. The *Every Child Matters* strategy (launched in 2003) was based on five outcomes linked to the development of the whole child and their character. Another initiative, the Social and Emotional Aspects of Learning (SEAL) programme, aimed to assist the development of social and emotional skills in schools, and was introduced as part of the Secondary National Strategy in 2007 (DfES, 2005). Although evaluations of both these initiatives were not entirely positive and both have now largely faded away, they did pave the way for the current interest in character education across both main political parties.

When Nicky Morgan succeeded Michael Gove as Secretary for State for Education in 2014 she made character education a central plank of her educational reforms. In her pledge to 'Step up to Serve', she highlighted the importance of character education by arguing:

> *Character education is part of our core mission to deliver real social justice by giving all children, regardless of background, the chance to fulfil their potential and achieve their high aspirations.*
>
> (www.iwill.org.uk/pledge/department-education/)

Nicky Morgan backed up this commitment by initiating the Character Awards for Schools. In 2015, 25 schools from regions across England were recognised for their efforts in character education. The awards were also designed to highlight the most effective ways that schools can develop character in their students. At the same time a new character education fund was established and designed to support and expand character education provision in schools. The Education Endowment Fund (EEF) also set up a fund to evaluate the impact of established character education programmes.

Importantly, character education has cross-party support. Tristram Hunt, the then Shadow Secretary of State for Education, foregrounded character education and stated that character virtues are vital components of a rounded education and good preparation for a career – and that instilling them in young people should not be left to chance (http://press.labour.org.uk/post/76422804073/schooling-for-the-future-speech-by-tristram-hunt). Hunt built his argument on the premise that there is growing evidence that character can be taught, and has cited academics including James Heckman and James Arthur as providing evidence for this. Character is also central to the *Curriculum for Excellence* in Scotland, implemented in schools in 2010–11. This curriculum aims to ensure that all children and young people in Scotland develop the attributes, knowledge and skills they will need to flourish in life, learning and work. The curriculum seeks to develop four key capacities – to be successful learners, confident individuals, responsible citizens and effective contributors – all of which have the development of core character virtues at their heart.

The term 'character' is also increasingly used by policy makers in contexts outside of education. For example in 2011, after the riots in England, the then Prime Minister David Cameron stated '*Education doesn't just give people the tools to make a good living, it gives them the character to live a good life, to be good citizens*' (https://www.gov.uk/government/speeches/pms-speech-on-education–2).

Furthermore, the Riots Commission Report recommended that every school should have a policy for character education (Riots Communities and Victims Panel, 2012). The main recommendation of the Riots Commission Report was that young people need to build character to help them realise their potential, and prevent them from making poor decisions, such as choosing to riot. The report also indicated that schools should assume responsibility for helping children build character. Likewise the all-party parliamentary group (APPG) on social mobility suggests that '*teaching "character and resilience" should be an essential part of every school's ambition and can be taught*' (Paterson et al., 2014). A Populus (Jubilee Centre, 2013) survey indicated parents think schools can, and should, teach character, and the CBI has called for character education to become a more conscious part of schooling (CBI, 2012). Character has been the subject of several large studies by the Jubilee Centre for Character and Virtues (Arthur et al., 2015) and the think tank *DEMOS* (Birdwell et al., 2015). One of the more important developments in character education has been the establishment of the Jubilee Centre for Character and Virtues. A multi-million pound institution at the University of Birmingham, the centre is a major international hub of interdisciplinary research into character, virtue and values education. Its vision is to conduct research that has both theoretical and practical implications. The launch of a centre of such size and ambition is a reflection of the increasing focus on character in Britain today.

International perspectives on character education

The trend towards character education is not just confined to the UK. Although character has been taught in some form in schools for hundreds of years, the modern renaissance of interest in the subject can perhaps be traced back to the United States in the 1980s (Arthur, 2003). Initially the impetus came from those in the conservative right who saw the potential for character education to restore a sense of order and improve behaviour in schools. In the years that followed, Democrat President Bill Clinton, however, also supported the character movement. The case for character education was also made by people concerned about a perceived reduced emphasis on moral and civic virtues in society more widely. The educational response to these concerns in the US has been both academic and practical. Major research and development centres, often combining both of these elements, have been set up, such as the Centre for Character and Social Responsibility at the University of Boston and the Centre for Character and Citizenship at the University of Missouri. The educational response has also been multi-disciplinary. For example, Peterson and Seligman (2004) have developed a large and well-known programme to investigate character strengths and virtues from a positive psychology perspective, and they have identified six key classes of virtue which they believe to be the foundations of human flourishing. These form the basis of the globally popular Values in Action (VIA) measures, as well as forming a major strand in the new movement of so-called 'positive education' which is meant to include the cultivation of character. An indication of this global interest is the international Positive Education Network (iPEN) which has recently been established (see www.ipositive-education.net). Other American writers, such as Ryan and Bohlin (1999), Jacobs (2001), Berkowitz (2012) and Snider (2013) have all written books about character education and schools. Distinguished academics such as Sandel (2010), Gardner (2011) and Annas (2011) have written about the place of 'virtue' in the modern world. Many of these American academics, amongst others, have called for a renewed consideration of practical morality, through a refreshed focus on character and virtue. This call is being realised in organisations such as the Knowledge if Power Programme (KIPP) schools, which are becoming world famous for their emphasis on character education. KIPP's motto is 'work hard and be nice' and this is central to their approach to character education. All the schools in the KIPP chain believe character alongside attainment is essential if their students are going to succeed. KIPP's character work focuses on seven character strengths that the founders claim, based on evidence, correlate to their students leading engaged, happy and successful lives. These strengths are: zest, grit, optimism, self-control, gratitude, social intelligence and curiosity. The KIPP approach has in turn spawned non-profit organisations such as the Character Lab.

Countries other than the US and the UK have shown an increased interest in matters of character education in recent years. Singapore, regularly held up as offering one of the best educations in the world and regularly at the top of the Program for International Student Assessment (PISA) tables, has recently adopted a new curriculum called 'Character and Citizenship'. This curriculum puts a strong emphasis on developing the character qualities of students alongside academic achievement – the belief is that the two go hand in hand. Japan is also part of this global trend. Recent moves by the Central Council for Education have introduced moral education as an official school subject, on a par with traditional subjects like Japanese. The council report states that moral education plays an important role in helping children realise a better life for themselves but also ensures sustainable development of the Japanese state and society. The motivation of the council appears to be clear – they believe that moral education can and should be taught more formally.

Other countries, such as India, China and Taiwan, have also introduced character education programmes of study, although the content and general tenor of these is different. Schools and local educational organisations and bodies in countries as far and wide as Canada, Korea, Australia and Malaysia have also had an increasingly recorded interest in character education. In the last few months, the Knightly Virtues Programme (see case study in Chapter 11), which teaches about moral character through stories and which is run by the Jubilee Centre for Character and Virtues, has been implemented in schools in the Netherlands, Russia, Peru, Canada, North America and Australia amongst others. This interest is perhaps symptomatic of the increasing global interest in teaching moral and other virtues through character education.

Why the renewed interest in character education?

So what has brought about this renewed interest in character education? There is no straightforward answer to this question as the agenda seems to have been driven by a number of concerns. The following list gives an overview of some reasons that have been given for the renewal of interest.

- A renewed focus on the link between character virtues and human flourishing (Kristjánsson, 2015; Arthur, 2003).

- Increased individualism leading to a loss of collective good character (Lasch (1991) and reduction in social capital (Putnam, 2000).

- Morality being eclipsed by individualistic economic and political frameworks (Wolfe, 2001; Bellah et al., 1996), leading to an increase in personal vice (Lickona, 1992).

- Capitalism and the market leading to a difficulty in developing values in a competitive age (Layard and Dunn, 2009) and the 'death of character' (Hunter, 2000).

- Young people not possessing the resilience or grit to succeed (Duckworth et al., 2007; Tough, 2012) or the mindsets that make a difference to aspirational achievement (Dweck, 2008).

- The increased focus on exams, measurement and testing at the expense of character (Seldon, 2013).

- Links between character, resilience and social mobility (Paterson et al., 2014).

- The link between non-cognitive skills and success after school (Kautz et al., 2014; Heckman and Rubinstein, 2001).

Whatever the reason for the renewed interest in character education, the move to develop an educational response has been largely driven by two disciplines – philosophy and psychology. The links between positive psychology, positive education, character, virtues, happiness and well-being have formed a major part of the response (see for example Peterson and Seligman, 2004). The other significant trend is the promotion of Aristotelian conceptions of virtue ethics as a recognised foundation for character education (see for example Arthur et al., 2015; Kristjánsson, 2015). Both of these trends will be discussed in more depth and in greater detail in Chapter 3.

Core message – FACT

The core messages in this book can be summed up in the acronym FACT. This stands for:

F – Flourishing

A – Adaptable

C – Caught

T – Taught

F – Flourishing

Throughout the book teachers are asked to think about the purpose of education. It is suggested that education should be about helping pupils to flourish and that, in order to flourish, attainment is not enough. Education should be just as much about preparing young people for the tests of life as a life of tests. This means teachers should focus on building character virtues (moral, civic, performance and intellectual – explained in Chapter 2) in their pupils alongside developing knowledge in particular subjects. Flourishing also demands that teachers should help their pupils develop practical wisdom: the ability to know what the right thing to do is, at the right time. Practical wisdom can be enhanced by teachers facilitating real life opportunities for their pupils to 'test' their characters as well as creating structured opportunities for them to reflect on their character and virtues.

A – Adaptable

There is no blueprint for character education. It is hoped that this book will provide inspiration for educators to develop their own approach to character education. This includes: school communities coming together to identify the core values of the school and how these inform its mission and ethos; choosing virtues to focus on that they feel their pupils most need; developing taught and caught approaches to character education that fit with the context (local, rural, faith-based, etc.) and restraints (expertise, resource) of their particular school.

C – Caught

Character is largely caught – not only in schools but in every context that children and young people live in – be it at home, with their friends, undertaking voluntary activities, etc. This means that the culture and ethos of the school community is essential to good character education. Central to this is the quality of staff/pupil relationships, which has implications for both teacher training and CPD as well as school leadership and management.

T – Taught

Character can also be taught. Teaching young people about character provides them with a language and tools for their own character development. It also gives time for pupils to develop their own rationale for why character is important. It provides space and time to think about their own character development as well as the moral dilemmas they face. Teaching character gives it a focus and a presence in the school – and raises its profile. Character education can be taught as a discrete subject but also through and within formal and less formal curricula.

Overview of the book

This book provides an overview of the major debates on character education and is aimed at primary practitioners. As such the book provides an overview of the educational theory and evidence behind the recent resurgence in character education. The book is also designed to provide practical advice for how the theory can best be applied in the primary classroom. The book is divided into four sections.

In the first part a background to character education is provided. This starts in Chapter 2, which describes what character and character education are, and, just as importantly, what character education is not. In this chapter a description of the different types of virtues that make up character are described – these are often considered the building blocks of character. Chapter 3 covers the theory behind character education and describes how different disciplines conceive of the subject. This includes a discussion on Aristotelian virtue ethics which is viewed by many as the best philosophical basis for the subject. Recent trends in psychology and positive education and well-being are also explored and there is also a section on the trials and tribulations of measuring character. Chapter 4, the final chapter in the section, deals with the 'can character be taught?' debate. It shows that character education might be best considered as more than 'just a subject' as it is both caught and taught.

Part 2 explores how character might be *taught* in primary schools. Two main areas for teaching character are considered here. Chapter 5 describes what a discrete taught course in character education might encompass and how this relates to other subjects such as PSHE and citizenship. Chapter 6 explains how character can be educated through and within other subjects such as English, maths, science and PE. Both these chapters provide practical advice and lesson ideas for ensuring that character education is a visible and conscious part of primary schooling. Part two closes with some consideration of how taught approaches to character education might be assessed and pupil progress evaluated in Chapter 7.

Part 3 examines how good character is *caught* in primary schools. There are four chapters in this part and each explores a different theme. Chapter 8 looks at the hidden curriculum and how to develop a whole-school approach to building character in pupils. Chapter 9 considers what makes a primary school teacher a character educator – as well as offering advice for ITT providers on preparing teachers for the role. Chapter 10 focuses specifically on the character-building potential of some well-known and less well-known extra-curricular activities. A discussion of strategies useful for character coaching and reflection is also included here. The last chapter deals with approaches to drawing on resources in the wider school community to support character education – including parents, the voluntary sector and business.

At the end of the book the Appendices contain some materials that will help teachers implement character education in their school. Appendix 1 is an audit of the book mapped against the Association of Character Education (ACE) principles. In addition, in Appendix 2, there are recommendations for teaching materials and programmes as well as other books, papers and reports on character education. The Framework for Character Education, developed by the Jubilee Centre and its partners, is also included in Appendix 3.

Chapter summary

This chapter has made a case for why character matters and why schools and primary school teachers are starting to take character education increasingly seriously. It provides an overview of recent trends in character education both in the UK as well as in many countries around the world. Throughout the chapter some of the bigger themes of the book are introduced. These include: the character taught/ character caught debate, and the different types of virtues that teachers and schools should be seeking to build in their pupils.

Further reading

Arthur, J. (2003) *Education with Character: The moral economy of schooling.* London: RoutledgeFalmer.

This book was one of the first to explore what a re-emergence of character education in Britain might look like. The book provides an excellent history of character education as well as considering what lessons should be learnt from America.

Birdwell, J., Scott, R. and Reynolds, L. (2015) *Character Nation: A DEMOS report with the Jubilee Centre for Character and Virtues.* London: Demos.

A concise and focused report providing the recent history of character education in the UK as well as making some well-conceived recommendations for policy makers and practitioners.

References

Arthur, J. (2003) *Education with Character: The moral economy of schooling.* London: RoutledgeFalmer.

Annas, J. (2011) *Intelligent Virtue.* Oxford: Oxford University Press.

Arthur, J., Kristjánsson, K., Walker, D., Sanderse, W. and Jones, C. (2015) *Character Education in UK Schools: Research Report.* Birmingham, University of Birmingham. Available from: www.jubileecentre.ac.uk/userfiles/jubileecentre/pdf/Research%20Reports/Character_Education_in_UK_Schools.pdf (accessed 8 December 2015).

Bellah, R., Madsen, R., Sullivan, W. M., Swidler, A. and Tipton, S. M. (1996) *Habits of the Heart: Individualism and commitment in American life.* Berkeley, CA: University of California Press.

Berkowitz, M. (2012) *Navigating the Semantic Minefield of Promoting Moral Development.* Available from: http://amenetwork.org/oped/ (accessed 13 April 2012).

Birdwell, J., Scott, R. and Reynolds, L. (2015) *Character Nation: A DEMOS report with the Jubilee Centre for Character and Virtues.* London: Demos.

Carr, D. Character in Teaching. *British Journal of Educational Studies*, 55 (4): 369–89.

CBI (2012) *First Steps: A new approach for our schools.* London: CBI. Available from: http://news.cbi.org.uk/reports/first-steps/first-steps-pdf/ (accessed 20 December 2015).

Children Schools and Families Committee (2009) *National Curriculum.* HC344.1, Vol. 1, 2009.

DfES (2005) Social and Emotional Aspects of Learning (SEAL): Improving behaviour, improving learning. Available from http://webarchive.nationalarchives.gov.uk/20110809101133/http://nsonline.org.uk/node/66394 (accessed 20 December 2015).

Dweck, C. (2008) *Mindset: How you can fulfil your potential.* New York: Random House.

Duckworth, A. L., Peterson, C., Matthews, M. D., and Kelly, D. R. (2007) Grit: Perseverance and passion for long-term goals. *Journal of Personality and Social Psychology*, 92 (6): 1087–101.

Gardner, H. (2011) *Truth, Beauty, and Goodness Reframed: Educating for the virtues in the twenty-first century.* New York: Basic Books.

Gardner, H. and Davies, K. (2014) *The App Generation.* New Haven, CT: Yale University Press.

Heckman, J. and Rubinstein, Y. (2001) The importance of noncognitive skills: Lessons from the GED Testing Program. *The American Economic Review,* 91 (2): 145–9.

Hunter, J.D. (2000) *The Death of Character: Moral education in an age without good or evil*. New York: Basic Books.

Jacobs, D. (2001) The Red Road: The indigenous worldview as a prerequisite for effective character education. *Paths of Learning: Options for Families and Communities*, 9: 20–7.

Jubilee Centre for Character and Virtues (2013) *A Framework for Character Education: Jubilee Centre parents' survey*. Birmingham: Jubilee Centre for Character and Virtues, University of Birmingham. Available from: http://jubileecentre.ac.uk/userfiles/jubileecentre/pdf/character-education/Populus%20Parents%20Study%20-%20short.pdf (accessed 1 December 2014).

Jubilee Centre for Character and Virtues (2015) *Teacher Education and Character Education*. University of Birmingham. Available from: http://www.jubileecentre.ac.uk/userfiles/jubileecentre/pdf/character-education/Statement_on_Teacher_Education_and_Character_Education.pdf

Kautz, T., Heckman, J., Diris, R., ter Weel, B. and Borghans, L. (2014) *Fostering and Measuring Skills: Improving cognitive and non-cognitive skills to promote lifetime success*. OECD. Available from: www.oecd.org/edu/ceri/Fostering-and-Measuring-Skills-Improving-Cognitive-and-Non-Cognitive-Skills-to-Promote-Lifetime-Success.pdf (accessed 8 December 2015).

Kristjánsson, K. (2015) *Aristotelian Character Education*. London: Routledge.

Lasch, C. (1991) *The Culture of Narcissism: American life in an age of diminishing expectations*. New York: W. W. Norton & Co.

Layard, R. and Dunn, J. (2009) *A Good Childhood: Searching for values in a competitive age*. London: Penguin.

Lickona, T. (1992) *Educating for Character: How our schools can teach respect and responsibility*. Bantam: Bantam Trade.

Peterson, C. and Seligman, M. E. P. (2004) *Character Strengths and Virtues: A handbook and classification*. Oxford: Oxford University Press.

Paterson, C., Tyler, C. and Lexmond, J. (2014) *Character and Resilience Manifesto*. London: All-Party Parliamentary Group on Social Mobility. Available from: www.centreforum.org/assets/pubs/character-and-resilience.pdf (accessed 12 October 2015).

Putnam, R. (2000) *Bowling Alone*. New York: Simon and Schuster Paperbacks.

Riots Communities and Victims Panel (2012) *After the Riots: The final report of the Riots Communities and Victims Panel*. London: The Riots Communities and Victims Panel.

Ryan, K. andBohlin, K. (1999) *Building Character in Schools*. San Francisco, CA: Jossey-Bass.

Sandel, M. (2010) *Justice*. London: Penguin Group.

Seldon, A. (2013) *Why the Development of Good Character Matters More Than the Passing of Exams*. The Priestly Lecture. Birmingham: University of Birmingham. Available from: www.jubileecentre.ac.uk/userfiles/jubileecentre/pdf/conference-papers/Priestley%20Lecture%20 on%20Character%20Jan%202013%20FINAL%20v2.pdf (accessed 8 January 2016).

Snider, S. (2012) *The Character Compass*. Cambridge, MA: Harvard Education Press.

Tough, P. (2012) *How Children Succeed: Grit, curiosity and the hidden power of character*. London: Random House.

Wolfe, A. (2001) *Moral Freedom: The search for virtue in a world of choice*. New York: W.W. Norton and Company.

2 *What is character education?*

In this chapter you will:

- learn what good character education is and is not;
- read an overview of the different types of character virtues that might be developed through character education;
- explore some key principles about how best to teach the subject;
- challenge some of the common concerns and misconceptions about character education.

What is character education?

Before we can consider what character education is, it is important first to establish what is meant by the term 'character'. Character is a contested term and has been variously defined. The word is often used synonymously with other terms including:

- **Non-cognitive skills**: a term that is strongly associated with the work of Nobel Prize-winning economist James Heckman. Heckman and Kautz (2013) analysed large data sets to show that attributes such as self-discipline and persistence – not just academic achievement – affected education, labour market and life outcomes. It is also the term preferred by the Education Endowment Foundation in the UK.

- **Soft skills**: a term often used by employers to describe a whole range of qualities desired in a young person – these might include things as diverse as being on time, being able to write a report and being presentable. The term is particularly vague.

- **Social and emotional skills**: a term fairly common in the classroom – especially after the multi-million pound SEAL initiative. The term is used to describe a set of 'skills' or perhaps attitudes and beliefs that help young people learn, whilst improving school climate and behaviour, as well as being useful for life and work more generally.

- **Twenty-first century skills**: a term less used in the classroom – but one that is increasingly being used in academic and policy circles. It is often used to describe attributes that are important for young people to develop to survive in the modern world – including information, media and technology skills.

For teachers it might seem that the difference between these terms is simply semantics – that they all mean something similar, or the same thing. However, on closer inspection although the language might be used synonymously, there are important conceptual differences between some of the terms. For example, it has been argued that the use of 'soft' in 'soft skills' devalues the importance of these qualities (Paterson et al., 2014); and furthermore, that character is best viewed as a subset of personality which is made up of 'hard' not 'soft' qualities (see Kristjánsson, 2015, p.5). Character cannot be non-cognitive, as the process of enacting the virtues takes a great deal of cognition or thought, and the virtues themselves involve judgements which are by their very nature cognitive. The term 'non-cognitive skills' is often employed in the primary classroom simply to differentiate character qualities from 'academic' qualities. A more appropriate term for such use might be 'non-cognitively tested', or 'non-examined' (see Kristjánsson, 2015).

Character is the preferred term used throughout this book as it describes fundamentally what makes us … us. Character describes a way of being rather than simply a set of competencies or skills that we can learn. Character is the virtues we possess and the habits we have incubated. As this book adopts a largely Aristotelian virtue ethical theoretical base (see Chapter 3), 'character' is also a central pillar of this philosophy. Understanding the roots of character in virtue ethical terms ensures that the language is rooted in a strong academic and theoretical tradition which provides real grounding for its use. Further justification for its use, if needed, is that character is a term increasingly being used in UK educational policy and practice discourse.

Character is used, in this book, as an umbrella term to describe a set of qualities or virtues that guide our behaviour and conduct (see Jubilee Centre, 2013). The term 'character education' relates to any educational activity, implicit or explicit, that encourages young people to develop character qualities or virtues. The 'whats' and the 'hows' of character education will be explored in more detail throughout this chapter and others – but it is important to draw out one particular element of this definition at this stage. Character education is both implicit and explicit. It is both caught and taught. It is therefore both a subject and not a subject. It is not something that can be taught, like maths or English, simply in the classroom by specialist trained teachers. Bernard Crick, the eminent political philosopher, described citizenship education as 'more than a subject' (Crick, 1998), and character education should be conceived in the same way. Part Two of this book details strategies and approaches for teaching character in the primary classroom – however, true character education is much more than a series of lessons on subjects relating to character. Primarily this is because character is caught as much (or more so) as taught. It is this point that makes character education at times seem intangible – it is often hard to actually 'see' it going on in schools. Many primary heads or teachers would struggle to show a visitor to their school their 'character education' provision – in fact as a visitor you might be more likely to notice if it is absent.

Character education is as much about how a school is set up (its core values and how these shape its ethos) than a simple series of lessons in the subject. As such character education might be said to be part of the fabric of the school. *Schools of Character* might be described like a stick of rock – cut through them anywhere and you will find character education going on either implicitly or explicitly. The following passage from the *Framework for Character Education* is particularly helpful in this regard:

> *Character virtues should be reinforced everywhere: on the playing fields, in classrooms, corridors, interactions between teachers and students, in assemblies, posters, head teacher messages and communications, staff training, and in relations with parents. They are critical in extracurricular activities and should translate into positive feelings and behaviour. The process of being educated in virtue is not only one of acquiring ideas. It is about belonging and living within a community – for schools are, together with the family, one of the principal means by which students grow in virtue.*
>
> (Jubilee Centre, 2013)

The building blocks of character – the virtues

The way that character education has been described above might for some teachers appear a bit vague. It makes character education seem like something that is hard to get hold of, something that is difficult to shape and mould. It is the building blocks of character – the virtues – that help to make character education tangible and real. Like the term 'character' the term 'virtue' is also contested and not popular with some people. It is also a term that has dropped out of common usage in many quarters. A variety of other terms are often used instead of virtue – these include:

- strengths

- qualities

- traits

- dispositions

- values

These terms are often used interchangeably and mean similar things to most people. Research with youth social action providers found that most of these did not like the term 'virtue', but that this dislike was largely for semantic rather than substantive reasons (Arthur, Harrison and Taylor, 2015). Kristjánsson (2015) has given thoughtful consideration to the lexicon of terms used instead of 'virtue' and although he is comfortable with some of the other terms, he argues that 'virtue' is the most useful due to its philosophical underpinnings. 'Virtue' is also seen as having more clout and clarity than 'values' as well as many of the other terms listed above (see Battaly, 2015). Furthermore, as a term, it perhaps has more substance than either 'qualities' or 'strengths'.

In this book 'virtue' is the preferred term, although at times it is used interchangeably with strengths and qualities. It is argued that virtue is an appropriate term to use as it is an important part of an Aristotelian conception of character as conceived in the theory of virtue ethics. Aristotelian inspired virtue ethics is experiencing a revival in moral philosophy globally (and explored in more detail in Chapter 3). In this philosophy, character virtues enable us to do the right thing, at the right time. Aristotelian conceptions of character education are not without challenges, but are arguably the most suited to address concerns teachers might have about character and provide a theory of change that makes a direct link from the education of virtues to human flourishing. Flourishing is the widely accepted goal of human life and therefore character education aims to inculcate the virtues necessary for humans not to only thrive as individuals but also for societies to thrive as a collective.

A sensible question at this point might be to ask why the development of virtues in pupils should be a teacher's concern. To answer this question it is important to adopt a maximal conception of education, as opposed to something more narrow like 'schooling'. If true and full education is about preparing young people for their futures, then the development of character virtues is a central part of this preparation. Society demands humans who are, amongst other things compassionate, courageous, resilient, honest and respectful. The benefits of developing virtues in pupils are, however, not simply long term, they can also be more immediate. Teachers and pupils want to work in ordered classrooms where people are well behaved, treat each other fairly, with respect and with care; where courage is demonstrated when learning, and where people are self-motivated and independent learners. These virtues are not only important qualities for young people to possess when they leave school, they are also important for them to possess whilst at school. Virtue ethicists will also argue that, in addition to their instrumental benefits, virtues are part and parcel of any life well lived.

Which virtues?

Having accepted the term 'virtue' (or found a substitute that is more comfortable for them) a teacher must ask 'what virtues should I seek to develop in my pupils'? This question is hotly debated by those interested in character education both in the UK as well as globally. One way to start to answer this question is to look at how the virtues might be classified. The Jubilee Centre suggests there are four types of virtues plus an intellectual meta-virtue called practical wisdom. These are:

- **Moral**: *virtues that enable us to respond well to situations in any area of experience.*

- **Performance**: *virtues that might also be considered psychological capacities, that can be used for both good and bad ends and which enable us to put moral virtues into practice.*

- **Civic**: *virtues and skills that are necessary for engaged and responsible citizenship.*

- **Intellectual**: *virtues that support learning, as well as to critically reflect on our own as well as other people's characters.*

- **Practical wisdom**: *A meta-virtue that moderates and enables all the others.*

(Jubilee Centre, 2013, p. 4)

There is a growing acceptance, in the UK, that this four-part classification is useful for teachers and other practitioners (Birdwell et al., 2015). An adoption of this classification also provides a framework by which to evaluate the variety of approaches to character. Each of these four types will be given more consideration below.

Moral virtues

Examples: courage, honesty, compassion, justice, humility, gratitude

Many argue that character education should be essentially a moral pursuit and therefore the moral virtues should be given the greatest emphasis (see for example Lickona, 1992; Arthur, 2003). These proponents argue that moral philosophy should underpin character education, and that there should be a revival of virtue ethics and of moral traditions emphasising the need to inculcate good habits in individuals in order for them to live moral and flourishing lives. The Jubilee Centre for Character and Virtues, whilst not rejecting the importance of the other types of virtues, prioritises the moral virtues as the most important and states:

Whilst human flourishing requires intellectual and civic virtues – as well as generic virtues of self-management, often known as enabling and/or performance virtues – it is the moral virtues that are the most central and important. This is because whilst performance virtues help individuals to succeed, moral virtues enable societies to flourish.

(Jubilee Centre, 2013, p. 3)

Continuing on this theme the Centre contends that:

> *Individuals can respond well or less well to the challenges they face in everyday life, and the moral virtues are those character traits that enable human beings to respond appropriately to situations in any area of experience. These character traits enable people to live, cooperate and learn with others in a way that is peaceful, neighbourly and morally justifiable. Displaying moral and other virtues in admirable activity over the course of a life, and enjoying the inherent satisfaction that entails is what it means to live a flourishing life.*
>
> (Jubilee Centre, 2013, p. 3)

This position is also defended by other well-known character education researchers and academics. These include Lickona (1992) and Ryan and Bohlin (1999) who both stress that character education should be essentially a moral discipline. Hunter (2000) is a strong proponent of the view that the term 'character' and the language of ethics and virtue need to be rescued, as in recent times character education has strayed too far away from being a moral endeavour. Hunter states: '*Character is not, as the psychologists would have it solitary, autonomous, unconstrained; merely a set of traits within a unique and unencumbered personality*' (Hunter, 2000, pp.15–16). The most basic element of character is '*moral discipline*' and '*its most essential feature is the inner capacity for restraint and the ability to inhibit oneself in one's passions, desires and habits within the boundaries of a moral order*'.

The New York Times journalist David Brooks (2015) in his book *The Road to Character* makes the distinction between 'résumé' virtues and 'eulogy' virtues. He suggests that 'résumé' virtues are the virtues that you include on your CV to help you get a job – in the main these will be performance virtues such as resilience and adaptability. In contrast, 'eulogy' virtues are those we want people to use to describe us at our funeral. These are largely moral virtues such as compassion, courage and being a loving and caring person. David Brooks argues that the pursuit of résumé virtues tends to dominate and in doing so, much of what matters and is important about life is forgotten.

Primary school teachers are emphasising and reinforcing moral virtues every day – whether this is done implicitly or explicitly. For example, Foundation and Early Years teachers might be particularly concerned with ensuring their pupils share and play fairly with each other, whilst Key Stage 2 teachers might be more concerned with ensuring their pupils show academic integrity in their work or humility on the sports pitch. It is probably the case that such 'moral instruction' is done without much thought – it is simply part and parcel of being a teacher.

Some primary schools do take a more explicit approach to the development of moral virtues. For example, hundreds of schools each year take part in the popular Thank You Film Awards and Thank You Letter Awards (see http://www.jubileecentre.ac.uk/544/projects/current-projects/thank-you-letter-awards) which actively encourage young people to think about the virtue of gratitude. By creating films and writing letters pupils are encouraged to think about for what and to whom they are grateful to. Likewise some schools make moral virtues the central planks of their whole-school character programmes – such as West Kidlington Primary School which focuses on a different moral virtue each month and Topcliffe Primary School which places moral virtues at the heart of their five keys to success framework.

Performance virtues

Examples: resilience, grit, teamwork, determination

The most direct challenge to those who promote the view that character education is essentially a moral discipline is to see character as concerning the development of what might be called performance or enabling virtues. These are the types of virtues which might most commonly be associated with terms such as 'non-cognitive skills', 'social and emotional skills', 'soft skills', 'emotional intelligence' or even 'skills for life and work'. One of the most well-known proponents of these types of virtues is Paul Tough, author of *How Children Succeed* (2013). The focus of this book is the virtues of 'grit' and 'resilience' and Tough is strongly in favour of a predominantly performance virtues-based approach to character development. The book draws on the work in the US of the Knowledge is Power Programme (KIPP) schools, which focus on the resilience and grit of their pupils. This programme has been particularly influential in the UK and increasingly schools are adopting similar approaches to the development of character. Well-known academics such as Carol Dweck (2008) have contributed to the debate about performance character virtues through a focus on growth mindsets. Growth mindset theory is based on the premise that many basic abilities can be developed through dedication and hard work. Dweck believes that you can teach growth mindsets and this contributes to motivation and productivity in different spheres. Likewise, Angela Duckworth advocates that schools focus on the development of grit and self-control in schools. For Duckworth these are the key traits that predict achievement – as grit is the tendency to sustain interest in and effort toward very long-term goals (Duckworth and Peterson, 2007) and self-control is the voluntary regulation of behavioural, emotional and attentional impulses in the presence of momentarily gratifying temptations or diversions (Duckworth and Seligman, 2005). In particular the focus on grit, and by association resilience, is becoming a more visible feature of many character education programmes in the UK. A visible example of this is the 'How to Thrive' programme which teaches the Penn Resilience Programme to UK teachers. To date, over 1,000 teachers have been trained, thereby reaching thousands of young people.

Similar approaches to the development of performance virtues have been advocated in the UK. For example DEMOS commenced an inquiry into character in 2009 and defined character as a set of capabilities that an individual may or may not possess. The 'Inquiry' report (Lexmond and Grist, 2011) found that the most important character capabilities for individuals to possess are application, self-direction, self-regulation and empathy – the first three of which might be described as performance virtues. These are clearly virtues that most primary teachers would be keen to develop in their pupils. A struggle for many teachers is how to encourage their pupils to work independently and therefore display the virtue of self-direction. Self-direction will enable pupils to think of their own solutions to problems rather than calling in help from a teacher or TA whenever they are stuck. Likewise, application is a skill that many teachers seek to encourage in their pupils, to help them to stick to a task and not give up, for example when they are struggling with a maths problem.

Whilst at the present time the main dichotomy appears to be between moral and performance virtues, two other important types of virtue might be considered important to character education.

Civic Virtues

Examples: service, volunteering, citizenship

Civic virtues might be described as the active, social expression of moral virtues such as compassion and courage. They are the virtues that should be encouraged in young people to help them to become active and engaged citizens. They are the types of virtues that many primary schools seek to promote through school councils, and charity and fundraising events. Most primary schools run regular whole-school events and activities that encourage pupils to experience opportunities through undertaking beneficial service for others. Developing civic virtues is also a core part of the (non-statutory) curriculum subject of citizenship education.

Primary schools are an excellent location (whether in class or through wider school activities) for young people to learn about and practise the virtues associated with positive civic participation. There are also direct benefits to wider society of developing civic virtues from an early age and in primary schools. From an early age pupils can learn about issues that affect their lives, be they local, national and international. Learning about these concerns can be excellent motivators for expression of civic virtues.

Intellectual virtues

Examples: practical wisdom, critical thinking, integrity, open-mindedness, resourcefulness, curiosity

Intellectual virtues are closely associated with learning and schooling environments. They are the virtues that are required for young people to pursue knowledge, truth and understanding. Some of these virtues might be seen as important by teachers to promote independent learning – such as curiosity and resourcefulness. Some might be seen as important to promote deeper learning – like critical thinking; and some for learning successfully with others – such as open-mindedness and cooperation. Finally, some will support honest learning such as integrity. When they come together, the intellectual virtues enable pupils to pursue new knowledge and information and engage critically with it.

The meta-virtue – practical wisdom

One other virtue perhaps best described as a meta-virtue is particularly important to an Aristotelian conception of character. This virtue is called phronesis, meaning practical wisdom. Practical wisdom helps pupils to put the other virtues into practice – as such it should be considered a moderating or enabling virtue. In some cases it might be required to help pupils choose between vice and virtue – for example, should they get involved in a playground fight, walk away from it or try to break it up. However, more often or not the virtue choices pupils make are not between good and bad but between two possible goods – and the 'right' decision depends on the context. For example, pupils often have to decide between loyalty to a friend or being honest to their teacher. Do they tell the teacher and 'grass' on their friend or not when they have done something wrong? It is the specific context (defined by many factors – social, historical, cultural, individual) that defines what is the right decision in this instance. Practical wisdom helps pupils make these everyday virtue judgements and decisions.

Practical wisdom is something that is built up over time and is always in development. It would be too much to expect primary school pupils to make the wise or right decision every time. In fact it would be too much to expect any of us to make the wise or right decision in everything we do. However, over time one would hope that pupils learn to deliberate on situations they find themselves in and make better judgements about what is the 'best' course of action in any given situation. This means that pupils must be given the opportunity to make mistakes and learn from them – and therefore careful coaching and encouragement from teachers and other primary school staff is of great importance. Practical wisdom requires young people to look backwards and learn from past experiences, but also forwards to predict the best course of action.

Table 2.1 shows how practical wisdom can be conceived as the moderator of the other four types of virtues.

What virtues should primary schools be developing?

An important question is which virtues are the most important for schools to develop in young people. This is a question that should occupy the minds of headteachers and teachers – particularly when they are developing or revamping their schools' mission and ethos statements. One place teachers might turn to for inspiration is the Department for Education.

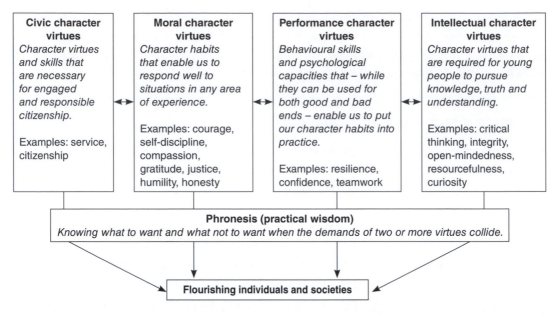

Table 2.1 Character virtues and phronesis (adapted from Jubilee Centre, 2013)

In 2015 the Department listed 21 character traits, attributes and behaviours that it believed underpinned success in education and work (see https://www.gov.uk/government/news/character-education-apply-for-2015-grant-funding). These are listed in Table 2.2, and have been split into the four types of virtues above for convenience.

Performance	Moral
• perseverance	• tolerance
• resilience	• respect
• grit	• honesty
• confidence	• integrity
• optimism	• dignity
• motivation	
• drive	
• ambition	
Civic	**Intellectual**
• neighbourliness	• conscientiousness
• community spirit	• curiosity
	• focus

Table 2.2 Department for Education priority virtues by type

The Department for Education has steered away from making any pronouncements on which character virtues from this list or any other that individual schools should prioritise. Teachers might also take inspiration from other well-known virtue lists such as the Values in Action (VIA) classification. This was developed by Peterson and Seligman (2004), who describe it as a comprehensive typology of character virtues, which consists of six virtues – wisdom, courage, humanity, justice, temperance, and transcendence – identified as core characteristics valued by moral philosophers and religious thinkers across time and world cultures. Out of each of these six virtues emerge a further four associated strengths of character – making a list of 24 in all. Peterson and Seligman have developed a free, online, self-report survey which enables individuals to generate a profile of their 'signature strengths', i.e. the five character strengths or virtues they display most frequently on a daily basis. Although the measure relies on self-reporting, it is an interesting tool to encourage pupils (and teachers) to think about their own character strengths and weaknesses. There is a specially designed version for children and young people (10–17 years old) with fewer questions which would be appropriate for Years 5 and 6. The VIA can be accessed for free here: www.viacharacter.org/www/The-Survey.

It should be questioned whether or not it is desirable, or indeed even possible, to identify a list of what might be called 'master' virtues that all schools should develop. One challenge to this comes from MacIntyre (1981, p.181), who has argued that '*there are just too many different and incompatible conceptions of a virtue for there to be any real unity to the concept or indeed to the history*'. Likewise, but less radically put, the Jubilee Centre (2013, p.3) believes that: '*No definitive list of relevant areas of human experience and the respective virtues can be given, as the virtues will to a certain extent be relative to individual constitution, developmental stage and social circumstance*'. The Centre recommends therefore that schools should develop their own list of core virtues that reflects the priorities of the young people and the communities they serve. It might be that some pupils really need a focus on resilience whereas for others issues such as cyber-bullying make a focus on compassion a more immediate concern. A focus on what might be argued are more 'universal' character virtues also might sit more comfortably with teachers concerned with the drive towards British values. The government strategy on *British Values* states that all schools have a duty to '*actively promote*' fundamental British values (https://www.gov.uk/government/uploads/system/uploads/attachment_data/file/380595/SMSC_Guidance_Maintained_Schools.pdf). However, teachers might rightly ask what makes the values promoted in the strategy, including democracy, freedom of speech, mutual respect and tolerance exclusively British. The British Values strategy, although seemingly well meaning, has the potential to undermine itself if it does not get teachers on board. It also could be viewed as potentially divisive. A more acceptable approach for many would be a focus on the development of universal virtues such as compassion, tolerance, courage, humility and many others, in their pupils.

Two approaches are suggested below that primary school teachers could adopt when they are considering which virtues their school should prioritise.

Approach 1: Create a list of priority virtues

Start by canvassing the opinion of key stakeholders by questioning governors, parents, community partners and the pupils themselves. The virtues that are deemed to be the most important to these groups are compiled into a list. Satellite virtues, those that closely relate to the identified core virtues, could also be included.

If this approach is adopted it is important that all four types of virtues are represented in the final list. This will give the list balance and ensure that the school is making a public statement that they want to educate pupils who will succeed as individuals but also pupils who will play a full, positive and beneficial role in society more generally. It is also worth noting evidence from Seider (2102) who found, not surprisingly, through conducting in-depth, embedded research in schools, that the type of virtue they emphasised (be it moral, civic or performance) was the type the school was most successful at developing in their pupils.

Approach 2: Focus on developing practical wisdom

A different approach from that outlined above would be to eschew any exclusive list of virtues and instead recognise the unity of the virtues and focus on enhancing the practical wisdom of the pupils. This approach would involve identifying a working list of virtues that are considered to be beneficial to individual and societal flourishing. Rather than encouraging pupils to think about these separately, teachers should instead ask pupils to consider how they interplay with each other. The focus would be on helping pupils to make wise choices when virtue/vice or virtue/virtue dilemmas arise.

Rather than having a virtue of the week, schools that adopt this approach might instead have a weekly reflection session where the pupils think about when they have demonstrated practical wisdom (or not) when faced with a difficult dilemma.

Concerns and misconceptions about character education

Before turning to how character education and the development of the virtues might be put into practice in primary schools it is worth giving some attention to what is *not* character education or at least 'good' character education. Character education concerns some people as it is seen as a vehicle to promote the particular ideologies of any given teacher and/or school. It could be argued that many subjects would fall foul to the same accusation – but there are perhaps particular concerns about how character education might be construed and delivered by some teachers.

The concerns raised about character education commonly include:

- It is indoctrinating – some approaches to character education might involve teachers telling pupils how to behave in specific areas that are not in keeping with the modern pluralistic world of today. The underlying fear is that the subject is conservative and paternalistic – harking back to a golden age, and not about looking forward to meet future challenges.

- That it is about the promotion of one religion or religion more generally.

- That it is the job of parents not schools.

- That schools should focus on attainment and not character as there is no time or space to do both.

Much work has been done by academics (see Jubilee Centre, 2013) and practitioners (Morris, 2015) to reclaim character education from naysayers by laying to rest the concerns presented above. These concerns have been called 'myths' (Kristjánsson, 2013) and need to be challenged if character education is going to be taken on board by primary school teachers. The 'myths' can been challenged in the following ways.

Character education should not be indoctrinating

If character education rests on an Aristotelian philosophy of virtue ethics then it should be about helping young people make wise choices when confronted with dilemmas. It is not about telling pupils what to do, or what to think (although guidance is of course important), but about providing them with opportunities and experiences that help pupils to develop their practical wisdom. At the heart of character education is enhancing pupils' ability to reflect critically on the situations and dilemmas they face. They need to learn to reflect upon and question their own actions and decide themselves what the 'right' thing is to do. The Jubilee Centre contends that moral character education, when taught in a particular way, need not be indoctrinating as it is about *'helping students grasp what is ethically important in situations and to act for the right reasons, such that they become more autonomous and reflective'* (Jubilee Centre, 2013). The ultimate goal of all proper character education is to equip students with the intellectual tools to choose wisely of their own accord within the framework of a democratic society.

Character education, undertaken well, is therefore not about being paternalistic or indeed conservative. It should be about building character strengths in pupils that help them meet modern and future challenges. The motivation for schools to adopt character education should not therefore be based on a desire to 'fix the kids' based on, say, a desire to return to Victorian values.

Character education is not necessarily religious

One of the more interesting and potentially controversial issues to unpack is the relationship between religion and character education. Many, in fact most, major religions would subscribe to the development in young people of the moral virtues described above. However, this does not mean that character education must rest on religious foundations. Virtue ethics philosophy, as described through much of this book, also provides a strong foundation from which to develop character education teaching and learning approaches. Adopting a virtue ethics framework allows teachers to sidestep questions they might find uncomfortable about the promotion of a religious viewpoint.

However, it would be wrong to deny that many faith schools see the development of character virtues as at the heart of their mission and ethos. In fact in many religious schools, of all faiths and denominations, the use of explicit virtue language is common. This is of course in keeping with Catholic, Church of England, Muslim, Jewish, Sikh or Buddhist and other religious teachings. Interestingly, evidence drawn from the trial of the Knightly Virtues Programme demonstrated that pupils who attended faith-based primary schools have higher virtue literacy (understood as a knowledge and understanding of virtue terms) than those who attended non-religious schools (Arthur et al., 2014). The explanation for this result might be because pupils attending faith schools are more likely to encounter virtue language in their daily interactions – for example through assemblies, school displays, prayer sessions or preparation for religious rites of passage such as first communion.

The important point, however, is that character education does not have to be religious. When viewed through a virtue ethical lens, it is about the development of a set of core, universally acknowledged virtues that are not necessarily tied to any particular religion or culture and are generally held by society to be good and right. This means that all teachers should be able to find a way into the subject – whether they are religious or not.

Character education is not just the responsibility of parents

Chapter 11 includes a section on how teachers and parents can partner on character education. Rightly, most people believe that parents should be primarily responsible for the character of their sons and daughters. Character has traditionally been viewed as the preserve of parents. However, although this should clearly be the case it is perhaps short-sighted to argue that schools should not have any role. There are two good reasons why perhaps they should. The first reason is the oft-cited statistic that pupils spend a great deal of their lives in schools and therefore the reality is that teachers are 'in loco parentis'. However, a second more positive reason is that schools offer real opportunities for pupils to develop character. Sometimes, these are opportunities not always available to pupils at home. For example, school trips away that help develop teamwork, collaboration amongst peers on a charity project and the host of extra-curricular activities that schools offer their pupils. Interestingly a Populus poll (Jubilee Centre, 2013) found very strong support among parents for the idea that schools should be promoting development alongside academic study. Eighty-seven per cent of the parents questioned felt that schools should focus on character development, and 84 per cent of parents thought that teachers should encourage good morals and values in their students. Furthermore, 81 per cent of parents wanted their son's/daughter's school to have a core statement on the values that it wants to instil in its pupils.

Education should be about attainment AND character

The role of schools is regularly questioned. After all, teachers can only do so much. Is it fair to expect teachers not only to be responsible for making their pupils achieve academically but also for building their character? It might be argued that as many teachers are overworked and there is only so much time in the school day a school should prioritise attainment over character. Recent educational policies have helped (both explicitly and implicitly) to strengthen this view. The narrow focus on grades, attainment and progress in school league tables and by schools inspectorates, means that schools are disproportionately judged on how their pupils perform in tests and exams. This has given rise to a widespread belief that schools are becoming exam factories.

This returns us to the question of the purpose of education. Should schools simply be preparing their pupils for a life of tests or in fact is it more important that a full education is about preparing them to meet the tests of life? One danger with placing the spotlight so heavily on attainment is that (perhaps as an unintended consequence) the curriculum is narrowed. Activities that are judged to directly improve attainment are prioritised over those that might be seen as a distraction. For example, it is not uncommon to visit schools that have either reduced curriculum time for subjects such as PSHE in order to provide maths top-up classes, or that have marginalised extra-curricular activities in order to provide 'interventions' to improve exam results. This swap may have been made based on good intentions, but the unintended consequence is that opportunities to develop character virtues through playing chess, or learning a musical instrument, or participating in an environment club have been lost.

There is another way to consider the attainment/character conundrum – to flip it on its head and ask how good character can contribute to attainment. Trials, primarily undertaken in America, have provided evidence about the positive effect of character education on attainment (see, for example, Berkowitz and Bier, 2006). The Educational Endowment Foundation is also conducting similar trials in 2015/16. However, many teachers do not need such evidence to see the link between character and academic achievement. It is clear that many character qualities are prerequisite in good learners. To be a good learner you need to be persistent, courageous, ordered, motivated and independent. The case perhaps needs to be made with more conviction that character education rather, than distracting from attainment, actually benefits it. Furthermore, if you focus on character pupils will also gain so much more besides.

Anthony Seldon, the former Master of Wellington College, gave an impassioned plea that character education should come before attainment by arguing that the pendulum had swung too far in one direction. In an open letter to Michael Gove (the then Secretary of State for Education) and Michael Wilshaw (head of Ofsted) he stated

> *Why then do I say that schools should prioritise character-building above exams? Because if you prioritise exams in the way that you are both doing, Michael and Michael, little or nothing will happen with character. But if you prioritise character, exam success will follow, and for the right reasons. The students will behave well in class. They will respect their teacher and each other. They will want to learn, rather than being made to learn. They will want to behave rather than being made to behave. They will probe beneath surface learning to the depths of subjects because they will be more reflective people.* (http://www.birmingham.ac.uk/Documents/college-social-sciences/ education/events/priestley-2013-anthony-seldon.pdf p13)

As will be explained in detail later in this book, character education can and should be taught through and within all curriculum subjects. It should not distract from the core curriculum, but reinforce and complete it. For example, stories in English make great opportunities to discuss character virtues of the heroes and heroines (see Carr and Harrison, 2015).

This book promotes a modern positive conception of character education – one we believe would be acceptable to most primary teachers in Britain. It is a type of character education that should prove attractive to primary schools across the country – be they be faith or non-faith based, independent or state, rural or urban, rated outstanding or in special measures by Ofsted. Indeed, extensive empirical research into character education in UK schools has demonstrated all schools have the potential to become schools of character (Arthur et al., 2015).

Chapter summary

This chapter has attempted to answer the question what is character? It has started by considering the semantic and substantive differences between other terms such as soft skills and non-cognitive skills. Next, the chapter considered the building blocks of character of the virtues. It was argued that the virtues are best conceived of in four types: moral, civic, performance and intellectual. Schools should try to develop virtues from across all these types in their pupils if they want both for them to flourish as individuals and for wider society to flourish. Two approaches were suggested for schools looking for strategies to decide which virtues they should prioritise. The final section of the chapter focused on some of the well-known challenges and misconceptions about character education. A defence was given for the subject from those who argue that it is indoctrinating, promoting of religion, distracting from attainment and the job of parents not teachers.

Further reading

Brooks, D. (2015) *The Road to Character*. New York: Penguin Random House.

This book, written in a very accessible style by the New York Times journalist, explores the difference between eulogy virtues and résumé virtues. Brooks explains that résumé virtues are the ones we strive to get to be successful in our careers. It is the eulogy virtues (what people say about us when we die) that really matter.

References

Arthur, J., Harrison, T., Carr, D., Kristjánsson, K. and Davison, I. (2014) *Knightly Virtues: Enhancing Virtue Literacy Through Stories*. Research Report. Birmingham: University of Birmingham, Jubilee Centre for Character and Virtues. Available from: www.jubileecentre.ac.uk/1545/projects/ development-projects/knightly-virtues (accessed 8 December 2015).

Arthur, J. (2003) *Education with Character: The moral economy of schooling*, London: RoutledgeFalmer.

Arthur, J., Harrison, T. and Taylor, E. (2015) *Building Character – through Youth Social Action*. Birmingham: University of Birmingham. Available at: http://www.jubileecentre.ac.uk/1574/projects/previous-work/character-and-service (accessed 9 December 2015).

Battaly, H. (2015) *Virtue*. Cambridge: Polity Press.

Berkowitz, M. W. and Bier, M. C. (2006) *What Works in Character Education: A research driven guide for educators*. Washington, DC: Character Education Partnership. Available from: https://characterandcitizenship.org/images/files/wwcepractitioners.pdf

Birdwell, J., Scott, R. and Reynolds, L. (2015) *Character Nation: A DEMOS report with the Jubilee Centre for Character and Virtues*. London: DEMOS.

Brooks, D. (2015) *The Road to Character*. New York. Penguin Random House.

Carr, D. and Harrison, T. (2015) *Educating Character Through Stories*. Exeter: Imprint Academic.

Crick, B. (1998) *Education for Citizenship and the teaching of democracy in school: Final report of the advisory group on citizenship*. London: Qualifications and Curriculum Authority.

Duckworth, A. and Peterson, C. (2007) Grit: Perseverance and passion for long-term goals. *Journal of Personality and Social Psychology*, 92 (6): 1087–101.

Duckworth, A. and Seligman, M. (2005) Self-discipline outdoes IQ in predicting academic performance of adolescents. *Psychological Science*, December, 16 (12): 939–44.

Dweck, C. (2008) *Mindset: How you can fulfill your potential*. New York: Random House.

Heckman, J. and Kautz, T. (2013) *Fostering and Measuring Skills: Interventions that improve character and cognition*. Cambridge, MA: National Bureau of Economic Research. Available from: http://www.nber.org/authors/james_heckman (accessed 9 December 2015).

Hunter, J. (2000) *The Death of Character: Moral education in an age without good or evil*. New York: Basic Books.

Jubilee Centre (2013) *Jubilee Centre Parents' Survey*. Birmingham: Jubilee Centre for Character and Virtues, University of Birmingham. Available from: http://jubileecentre.ac.uk/userfiles/jubileecentre/pdf/character-education/Populus%20Parents%20Study%20-%20short.pdf (accessed 8 December 2015).

Jubilee Centre (2013) *Framework for Character Education*. Birmingham: University of Birmingham. http://jubileecentre.ac.uk/userfiles/jubileecentre/pdf/other-centre-papers/Framework.pdf (accessed 8 December 2015).

Kristjánsson, K. (2015) *Aristotelian Character Education*. Abingdon: Routledge.

Lexmond, J. and Grist, M. (eds) (2011) *The Character Enquiry*. London: DEMOS.

Lickona, T. (1992) *Educating for Character: How our schools can teach respect and responsibility*. New York: Bantam.

MacIntyre, A. (1984) *After Virtue* (2nd edn). Notre Dame, IN: University of Notre Dame Press.

Morris, I. (2015) *Teaching Happiness and Wellbeing in Schools: Learning to ride elephants* (2nd edn). London: Bloomsbury.

Paterson, C., Tyler, C. and Lexmond, J. (2014) *Character and Resilience Manifesto*. The All-party Parliamentary Group on Social Mobility. Available from: http://www.centreforum.org/assets/pubs/character-and-resilience.pdf (accessed 12 October 2015).

Peterson, C. and Seligman, M. E. P. (2004) *Character Strengths and Virtues: A Handbook and Classification*. Oxford: Oxford University Press.

Ryan, K. and Bohlin, K. (1999) *Building Character in Schools*. San Francisco, CA: Jossey-Bass.

Seider, S. (2012) *Character Compass: How powerful school culture can point students towards success*. Cambridge, MA: Harvard Education Press.

Seldon, A. (2013) *Why the Development of Good Character Matters more than the Passing of Exams*. The Priestly Lecture. Birmingham: University of Birmingham. Available from: www.jubileecentre.ac.uk/userfiles/jubileecentre/pdf/conference-papers/Priestley%20Lecture%20on%20Character%20Jan%202013%20FINAL%20v2.pdf (accessed 8 December 2015).

Tough, P. (2012) *How Children Succeed: Grit, curiosity and the hidden power of character*. London: Random House.

3 Character education: theory and measurement

In this chapter you will:

- be provided with an overview of theories of flourishing from philosophical and psychological perspectives;
- consider in depth the Aristotelian notion of virtue ethical theory and gain an understanding as to why it provides a useful foundation for character education;
- explore the links between character education, positive psychology and positive education;
- consider the challenges of measuring character.

Introduction

It has been argued in the previous chapters that character education contributes to individual and societal flourishing – and therefore it should be the concern of all teachers and schools. But what is the theoretical basis for this claim? Attempting to find answers to the fundamental question 'what makes us flourish' is the concern of several academic disciplines. The sciences and the arts, for example, would have much to say about what helps humans to flourish (e.g. work on physical and mental health, or the importance of aesthetic beauty and artistic expression for a happy and meaningful life). However, in the UK, as well as elsewhere, character education has largely been researched in the disciplines of philosophy and psychology. This chapter provides an overview of how these academic disciplines have contributed to the debate about the theoretical basis for character education. It concludes with a discussion about how character might be measured and the challenges associated with doing so.

Philosophy

The father of character education, for many, is the ancient Greek philosopher Aristotle. Virtue ethics, the moral philosophy Aristotle is most closely associated with, is increasingly being viewed (at least in western countries) as providing the most suitable theoretical foundation for character education (see Kristjánsson, 2015). More generally, virtue ethics and an emphasis on character and virtue, is now viewed as a viable alternative to the previously popular moral theories of deontology and utilitarianism.

Virtue ethics, deontology and utilitarianism

The question of how best to lead a moral life is one of the foundational questions of philosophy. Moral philosophers have, over the years, formulated theories designed to help people make the best moral decisions. Historically, many moral theories have been developed by philosophers and the three most widely accepted and therefore most prominent are deontology, utilitarianism and virtue ethics. It is virtue ethics, in recent times, that has been viewed as the most promising basis for character education. Whereas deontology emphasises rules and duties for doing the right thing, and utilitarianism is based on making a calculated assessment of consequences as guidance for doing the right thing, virtue ethics emphasises the character virtues of individuals as the basis for making good and wise decisions. Virtue ethics has undergone a resurgence – in particular in the UK since the influential article 'Modern Moral Philosophy' by Elizabeth Anscombe (1958) was published. Anscombe was critical of ethical theories that prioritised one's duty and obligation, suggesting instead that moral theorising should be based on notions such as character and virtue. Since this paper appeared, a renaissance of virtue ethics has been seen across the disciplines. These include most notably:

- Moral philosophy and, in particular, the work of Alasdair Macintyre (1981) who, in his most well-known book, *After Virtue*, argues that moral discourse within modern society is dysfunctional and articulates a politics of virtue to protect from the corrosive effects of the capitalist economy.

- In moral psychology and in particular the work of Peterson (2006) and Seligman (2011) who devised a framework called the VIA of character strengths, which sets out the psychological ingredients for displaying human goodness, serving as pathways for developing a life of greater virtue.

- In moral education and the work of James Arthur (2003) amongst others who have sought to develop educational approaches based on virtue ethical theory.

Aristotelian conceptions of character

The origins of virtue ethics can be traced back to the writings of Plato but are more significantly located in the philosophy of his student Aristotle (384BC–322BC). Several concepts central to the way Aristotle understood ethics are also important components of modern virtue ethical theory. These concepts are outlined by Aristotle in one of his most influential works, the *Nicomachean Ethics.* Three concepts in particular make up the central pillars of virtue ethics and are also useful for framing theoretical arguments about the basis for character education. These are: *eudaimonia* (happiness or flourishing), *arete* (excellence or virtue) and *phronesis* (practical or moral wisdom).

Eudaimonia

Aristotle thought the supreme good or the end goal for all humans is *eudaimonia*, which is traditionally translated as either *happiness* or *flourishing*. It is both the most complete end and also a self-sufficient end because it cannot be improved by any other good. *Eudaimonia* – living and acting well and flourishing – was for Aristotle the goal of all human life. Happiness is equated to virtuous activity of the soul, rather than it being something we achieve when certain circumstances are met; in other words, happiness is the activity of doing something in an excellent way, it is not a passive state which arises when certain conditions such as money, fame, health or pleasure are met. Happiness derives from the living of a life, rather than the circumstances of a life (Annas, 2011). In *Nicomachean Ethics*, Aristotle sought to understand the nature of a flourishing life and in particular, what components make up such a life and what control, if any, an individual has over it. He rejected the view that flourishing was about a life of sensual pleasure. Instead, for Aristotle, a flourishing life is about contemplation and the possession and practice of the virtues. The purpose of character education therefore, is to contribute to the flourishing life which enables individuals as well as societies to flourish.

Arete (virtue or excellence)

The key to Aristotle's ethics and understanding of what it means to flourish is *arete*, often understood as excellence or virtue. A person with *arete* is a person of the highest moral effectiveness; they have all the virtues for a good life. Aristotle believed that virtues were 'states of character' rather than passions or facilities. In *Nicomachean Ethics*, Aristotle writes

We must consider what virtue is. Since things found in the soul are three kinds – passions, faculties, states of character – virtue must be one of these. By passions I mean appetite, anger, fear, confidence, envy, joy, friendly feeling, hatred, longing, emulation, pity and in general the feelings that are accompanied by pleasure or pain; by faculties the things in virtue of which we are said to be capable of feeling these, e.g. of becoming angry or being pained or feeling pity; by states of character the things in virtue of which we stand well or badly if we feel it violently or too weakly, and well if we feel it moderately.

(Translated in Darwell, 2003, p.17)

Aristotle believed that people should aspire to moral virtues and be educated for 'excellence of character'. Darwell (2003, p.12) explains that the virtues, for Aristotle, were dispositions to choose what is fine or noble for its own sake, and to avoid what is base. Badhwar (1996, p.306) explains that *'Aristotle's conception of virtue of character is of a habitual emotional and rational disposition to feel, choose and act in the right way for the right ends'*. Aristotelian character is also, importantly, about a state of being. It is about having the appropriate inner states – as such emotion is central to Aristotelian philosophy. The education of the emotions is an important part of character education.

Virtue, for Aristotle, is found in the middle ground between a deficiency and an excess of appetite, passion or desire. This influential idea is often referred to as *'the doctrine of the mean'*. The central premise of the doctrine is that moral qualities are destroyed by a deficiency or excess of any particular passion or emotion.

> *It is possible, for example, to feel fear, confidence, desire, anger, pity, and pleasure and pain generally, too much or too little; and both of them are wrong. But to have these feelings at the right times on the right grounds towards the right people for the right motive and in the right way is to feel them to an intermediate, that is to the best, degree; and this is the mark of virtue.*
>
> (Aristotle, 1976, p.101)

An example that Aristotle (1976, p.94) gives of the mean is that of courage, which regulates the emotion of fear: too little fear might lead to being foolhardy and too much fear to cowardice. The point where the mean is found varies with every given situation. As Hursthouse (1999, p.12) explains, in the case of generosity: *'this would involve giving the right amount of help, for the right sort of thing, for the right reasons, to the right people, on the right occasions'*. Importantly, Aristotle was influenced by Plato's belief that virtue was knowledge about what was good. However, he believed that it was not enough for people just to know what is good, they also had actually to be trained to be good.

In *Nicomachean Ethics*, Aristotle (1976) wrote that virtues are developed through habit and so there is a requirement for individuals to constantly practise them. He stated: *'we become just by performing just acts, temperate by performing temperate ones, brave by performing brave ones'* and that *'the moral virtues are neither by nor contrary to nature; we are constituted by nature to receive them, but their full development in us is due to habit'* (1976, pp.91, 92). As Sandel (2010, p.198) explains, *'Aristotle's emphasis on habit does not mean he considers moral virtue a form of rote behaviour. Habit is the first step in moral education'*. An important later part of character education is to seek to develop a moral autonomy and agency guided by reason in pupils. The first stage of this is the inculcation of good habits, which then moves to autonomy. Realistically, most primary school teachers are going to be more involved in the habituation stage, in preparation for more autonomy, but that does not mean that they are not also instrumental in helping pupils develop their budding practical wisdom.

Phronesis (practical moral wisdom)

A final important component of Aristotle's understanding of ethics, which forms a central part of modern day virtue ethics, is *phronesis*. Translations of *phronesis* have included, amongst others, practical reasoning, practical wisdom, good sense, moral discernment, moral insight, and prudence (Noel, 1999). Aristotle (1976) defines *phronesis* as a state of grasping the truth, involving reason, concerned with action that is good or bad for a human being. As has been previously discussed, virtues are more than tendencies to act in certain predetermined ways; they are excellences of character, which involve getting things right. For Aristotle it is *phronesis* that helps individuals get things right, as practical or moral wisdom: it is what helps individuals to make the right judgement in any given situation. Aristotle understood that the requirements of different virtues can bring about conflict because they sometimes point to different courses of action.

However, he also believed that such conflict is only apparent as it may be resolved by those possessed of practical wisdom. Therefore, a brave person exercises practical wisdom when he judges that a given situation merits fear and decides how to respond correctly. The coward, in contrast, exercises no practical wisdom as he or she perceives an unthreatening situation as dangerous. The development of practical wisdom comes with time and through practice, Aristotle believed that knowing the best course of action would eventually become second nature. *Phronesis*, for Aristotle, is different from other forms of reason, such as *episteme* and *techne*. *Episteme* is scientific knowledge and concerns things that are necessarily true, and *techne* is craft knowledge, useful for finding an effective way to make a product. Neither of these are necessary moral virtues, as they might be used for good or bad ends. *Phronesis* is different, as it concerns using practical wisdom to make a virtuous decision in any given situation.

Character education, as understood by Aristotle and neo-Aristotelians, can be defined as the pursuit of developing practical wisdom in children and young people. As young peoples' lives involve making decisions in ethical situations, character education provides opportunities and guidance to help young people make a wise choice when faced with moral dilemmas. This is particularly the case when two or more virtues appear to collide. For example, many students at schools have to decide between being honest to their teacher and loyal to a friend when they have done something wrong. Character education is a deliberate and conscious attempt to help these students make a wise choice when such a dilemma occurs. The theory is that as students develop practical wisdom they will make wiser decisions.

The three central concepts outlined above provide excellent tools for primary school teachers interested in developing approaches to character education to work with. The use of a virtue ethical framework is seen by organisations such as the Jubilee Centre for Character and

Virtues as a good way to bring some order and coherence to the multiple approaches that might fall under the umbrella of character education. Character education, based on virtue ethics philosophy, is viewed by the Centre as the best approach to cultivating the virtues of character associated with common morality, enabling young people to become good citizens and lead good lives (see Arthur and Harrison, 2012). However, rather than adopting a die-hard, dogmatic attitude to Aristotle's original conception of virtue ethics, many moral philosophers today are naturalists and seek modern interpretations of the philosophy to fit with contemporary knowledge and understanding of the world. They are also open to empirical testing of the assumptions of virtue ethics, and a re-conceptualisation of some of the philosophy is necessary (see Kristjánsson, 2015). Much of this empirical work, in recent times, has been carried out by psychologists.

Psychology

Alongside philosophy, psychology has been at the forefront of the re-emergence of character education globally. Eminent psychologists such as Lawrence Kohlberg (1981) and Martin Seligman (2011) have been particularly visible in the field. Where the philosophers have been keen to provide some solid theoretical foundations for approaches to character education, the psychologists have studied the link between character and human psychology as well as being at the foreground both of developing models of moral character development and of developing empirical tests, scales and other methods to measure it.

Kohlberg is perhaps the best known of the modern moral educationalists. He is known for his stage theory of moral development. The theory is based on the assumption that as a society we need to develop autonomous individuals who can make and justify moral judgements rationally from an impartial point of view. Kohlberg identified six stages to how young people might develop morally. These stages are grouped into three phases – the pre-conventional, the conventional and the post-conventional. Levels one and two are seen in pre-school pupils where behaviour is determined by the consequences of actions. Pupils in stages 1 and 2 (pre-conventional) will be most concerned with punishment avoidance and obedience and also exchanges of favours for rewards; in stages 3 and 4 (conventional) there is a need to please others and an understanding of law and order; and, in stages 5 and 6 (post-conventional) is the importance of a social contract and finally a universal ethical principle where people answer to an inner conscience. Kohlberg believed that most primary school pupils are at stages 1 or 2. This moral development stage theory has been widely critiqued as, over time, little valid and robust empirical evidence has emerged to support it. There has also been a gap in the evidence supporting any link between moral reasoning and moral action (Blasi, 1980).

Building on Kohlberg, but responding to the criticisms, a neo-Kohlbergian approach has been developed – popularly known as the 'Four Component Model'. The model addresses the ways in which moral behaviour occurs, and provides a conceptualisation of successful moral functioning and the capacities it requires. The model was originally developed by James Rest (1986) but has had several incarnations and been further developed and researched by Steve Thoma (Narváez et al., 1999), among others.

At the heart of the model are four inter-related abilities that it is believed are required to be a moral individual. The components are not seen as lineal or in stages – but all interact with each other. They are also demonstrated through cognitive and affective behaviour interacting with each other – thinking and doing in combination. The four components in the model are:

- **Moral sensitivity**: the ability to identify and discern problematic situations with ethical dimensions.

- **Moral judgement**: the ability to move beyond recognising that ethical dimensions are present in a given situation to explore which line of action is morally justified.

- **Moral motivation**: the ability to prioritise moral over other personal values.

- **Moral character:** the ability to combine sensitivity, judgement and motivation to behave morally.

Moral character and competence is defined as having the strength of your convictions, having courage, persisting, overcoming distractions and obstacles, having implementing skills, and having ego strength (Nucci et al., 2014).

Other notable psychologists well-known in the character education movement are Marvin Berkowitz and Melinda Bier. Berkowitz and Bier (2014) strongly believe that it is important to establish 'what works' in character education and that all classroom and school practice should be based on evidence. Drawing on this research these authors have developed a model of what works for schools interested in rethinking or evaluating their character education provision. The model is called PRIME and the main features of it are detailed below. The full model and supporting evidence is laid out in a chapter by Berkowitz and Bier entitled 'Research based fundamentals of the effective promotion of character development in schools' (see Berkowitz and Bier, 2014) in the *Handbook of Moral and Character Education*.

PRIME MODEL

P – *Priority:* Schools first and foremost must make a choice to teach character. It must be a top priority.

R – *Relationships:* Classrooms should foster relationships between anybody and everybody; any combination is beneficial, from student-to-student, teacher-to-student, and cross-age buddying. *'Relationships are the elements upon which healthy schools and character are built.'*

I – *Intrinsic motivation:* Help students understand that there is personal, internal satisfaction from achieving goals and behaving properly. *'Unless students internalize moral values, they will be temporary.'*

M – *Modelling:* Because teachers and administrators should have built strong relationships with their students, educators can now leverage their role-model status not only to *talk* about character, but also to *show* character.

E – *Empowerment:* Rather than educators solving all the problems for students, empower students to make decisions for themselves. Giving them real-life, authentic problems to solve as a team helps foster real world decision-making skills.

Positive psychology

A branch of psychology that is increasingly being linked to character education is positive psychology. The positive psychology movement was launched by Seligman and Csikszentmihalyi in 2000. It was defined as the scientific study of *'what goes right in life, from birth to death and all stops in-between'* (Peterson, 2006, p.4). The movement is concerned with helping individuals find a greater meaning and purpose in life. For schools this might involve helping pupils develop capacities to be able to critically reflect and make judgements that lead to heightened self-awareness. The goal of this self-awareness is to lead to higher levels of flourishing. Flourishing might be viewed on a spectrum from individual well-being and happiness to societal thriving. For most positive psychologists, the aim should be to meet both ends of this spectrum through discovering approaches that enable us to live well. This creates a direct link to positive education – which is defined as an *'umbrella term used to describe empirically validated interventions and programmes from positive psychology that have an impact on well-being'* (Seligman *et al.*, 2009). McMahon (2006) calls it a young science with a long history grounded in Aristotle (see also David et al., 2013, pp.535–671). The objective of positive education is to help pupils understand positive emotions and provide tools that can enable pupils at both these levels to achieve *eudemonia* (White and Murray, 2014, p.14). This is where cross-over with character education happens, as it is about the development of specific virtues or values though character-based lessons (White and Murray, 2014).

As discussed in Chapter 2 much of the positive psychology movement has been focused on developing what were earlier classified as performance virtues such as resilience (Duckworth and Peterson, 2007) and grit (Dweck, 2008) and successful interventions such as the Penn Resiliency programme have grown out of them. Peterson (2006), a founding member of the positive psychology movement, believed that these virtues and others should not only be present within individual members of an institution but at the collective level so the institution itself has 'moral character'. He calls the 'good school' (2006, p.284) one that contributes to both academic excellence as well as moral fulfilment – and as such should have moral goals that guide pupils to be responsible and caring. This, for Peterson, meant going beyond a 'police school environment' to managing issues such as cyber-bullying by putting in place practices that build character and well-being.

A common positive psychology approach is to focus on strengths. Perhaps the best known of these, as discussed previously, is the Values in Action programme (VIA) – which is a framework of universal human character strengths and virtues. White and Waters (2014) contend that the *'framework is useful because it provides teachers and students with a language to discuss what is good about the people within the school and the school culture at large'* (p.114). Evidence is emerging that educational approaches that incorporate the VIA framework can have a positive impact on enjoyment and participation in school (Seligman et al., 2009) and hope and engagement (Madden et al., 2013). Another useful resource is *Using Positive Psychology to Enhance Student Achievement* by Tina Rae and Ruth MacConville (2015). The book, although primarily designed for secondary schools, presents a series of lesson ideas and plans for how to develop good habits in children and young people that could be adapted for a primary setting.

Cross-disciplinary approaches

Increasingly academics are looking outside their own discipline for help with answering the bigger questions about character and virtue. Every year the Jubilee Centre hosts an annual conference which is attended by academics from philosophical, psychological, theological, sociological and educational backgrounds. Some of the most interesting papers that come out of the conference (see www.jubileecentre.ac.uk for all the papers) are those that have looked at character from a cross-disciplinary perspective. For example, psychologists and philosophers have come together to consider the virtue of gratitude (e.g. Carr et al., 2016); and sociologists and philosophers have looked at social structure, relationships, identity and character (e.g. Walker et al., 2014). This has also had an impact on practitioners, such as Ian Morris (2015) who has re-worked his approach to well-being and happiness by underpinning it with an Aristotelian eudaimonic framework. It may well be that in time the most interesting approaches to discovering theoretical and practical approaches to character education will come out of such cross-disciplinary teams.

Measuring character

How to measure character is one of the biggest challenges facing researchers working in the field of character education. In Chapter 8 some suggestions are made about how a primary school might try to evaluate their character education provision and Chapter 7 includes advice for assessing taught approaches to character education. However, before attempting to implement these strategies it is important to understand the considerable challenges associated with measuring character. These challenges include:

- the difficulties of measuring actual behaviour change;
- prioritising what should be measured;

- understanding the purpose of measurement;

- deciding who should lead on measurement;

- the question of whether it is even possible to measure character.

A discussion of each of these challenges is presented below.

The difficulties of measuring actual behaviour change

Ideally a school making an explicit focus on character education would be interested in finding out if their activities and interventions are having a positive effect on the actual behaviour and attitudes of their students. Schools would want to know if their students are becoming, for example, more resilient, humble, compassionate, courageous and honest. However, measuring actual behaviour change is extremely difficult to do. The method that would probably be most suited to this type of measurement would be close observation studies of different individuals and cohorts of pupils conducted over a long period of time. However, this method is both resource heavy and time consuming and would also require some prior expertise. Scale would also be an issue, as the larger the sample of pupils being observed the more valid the findings are likely to be. Research projects on this size and scope are beyond most primary schools, or indeed even universities.

It is for this reason that little empirical research into character education has focused on attempts at measuring actual behaviour change. One way to get at behaviour change might be to factor in proxy measures such as pupil attendance, behaviour, exclusions and attainment. An improvement in any of these metrics might signify that a school's approach to character education is working – however, it would be very hard to isolate which activities are having the most impact without running a randomised control trial. Trials of this nature have been conducted and, although the results are mixed, there is evidence that demonstrates that character education does have a positive effect on attainment, behaviour and other whole-school concerns (see Benninga et al., 2003). The Education Endowment Foundation have run similar trials which are reported on their website – see https://educationendowmentfoundation.org.uk/apply-for-funding/character-and-education-funding-round.

Due to the challenges outlined above, much research into the impact of character education has focused on more modest goals. For example, the Jubilee Centre has constructed research strategy, methods and tools to successfully measure what it calls *virtue literacy* (Arthur et al., 2014) – which is the knowledge and understanding of virtue terms and concepts.

How do we measure all the different types of virtues?

In Chapter 2 it was suggested that schools should choose which character virtues (be they moral, civic, performance or intellectual) they should prioritise the development of in their pupils. Choosing which virtues to focus on should be considered a relatively simple task compared to constructing a bespoke measure that would enable a school to 'test' how their pupils are progressing against each of them. It is for this reason that some schools rely on 'off the shelf' scales that purport to measure one of their priority virtues. Popular off the shelf scales tend to measure performance virtues such as teamwork, leadership and resilience. There are also some useful scales aimed at measuring intellectual virtues – such as the Myself as a Learner Scale (Burden, 2014). Although these scales tend to suffer from an over-reliance on pupils reporting their own character strengths and weaknesses, many will provide a reasonable picture of how any particular pupil rates themselves. Fewer tools exist for measuring moral and civic virtues in primary school pupils. This is due to the fact it is hard to develop accurate measures of compassion, gratitude, honesty, service and humility. A challenge for schools is to value equally all the different types of virtues they are seeking to develop as opposed to just those that appear easier to measure.

What is the purpose of measurement?

Some schools might for ideological or other reasons actually be opposed to attempts at measuring the character of their pupils. Schools are increasingly and legitimately complaining about the measurement regimes they are currently subjected to. Schools are often judged on fairly easy to obtain metrics such as exam scores and attendance that can be compiled into so-called league tables. It would be much harder to measure how a school develops the character of pupils and put this in an easily comparable table. However, as has been previously argued, parents, teachers, pupils, employers and many others value character just as much as attainment. In fact it would be easy to make a strong case that an over-emphasis on measurement, particularly of attainment, has squeezed out character education provision in many schools. Schools, under the measurement cosh, resort to narrow strategies that seemingly improve attainment in pupils rather than more expansive activities that build character. It is often said that schools spend too much time preparing young people for a life of tests rather than the tests of life. It is for this reason that schools are right to be cautious about measuring character and first ask the important question - what is the purpose of doing so?

There are a number of justifiable purposes for measuring character. One purpose might be to build up a picture of the collective character of a school for developmental purposes. This picture would help teachers see where pupils' strengths are and where more effort, resources and time need to be directed. This approach might be described as taking the 'temperature' of character in a school. If such an approach is to be considered, schools should be careful not to focus the aim of the measurement on individuals' strengths and weaknesses, but instead seek to combine and aggregate (ideally anonymous) scores to view patterns across the school, or perhaps a year group or classes. Another purpose might be to evaluate the effectiveness of a new character education intervention being brought into the school – to discover 'what works'. To do this well an experimental trial is most probably required – which as argued earlier would be beyond the scope of most schools. However, lighter touches to evaluation would also be useful. These might include teachers peer observing and feeding back on lessons or activities, or running focus groups with pupils to obtain qualitative data that would shine a light on what impact a new intervention is having.

Who leads on measurement?

A difficult question, which relates to the purpose discussion above, is who should actually develop the principles, frameworks, methods and tools required for effective measurement of character? As has been suggested above it would be beyond the scope of most schools to develop new character measures, let alone have the capacity or indeed expertise to implement them. However, many primary schools may be opposed to top-down measures enforced by the government and perhaps inspected by Ofsted. Another option would be to involve universities, yet although some work has been done in this regard by researchers few have the capacity or resources to tackle this problem on a large scale.

Is it even possible to measure character?

Perhaps the biggest challenges to measuring character are methodological (Kristjánsson, 2015, Chapter 3). To date there is no measure of any character virtue popularly available that does not suffer from some challenges to its validity. Even highly sophisticated instruments and tools that are implemented and the data analysed by experts in the field are also often questioned. The simple truth is that it is extremely difficult to develop an effective strategy for measuring character that can be defended against all validity claims.

Most popular scales that are currently readily available rely on individuals self-reporting on their character strengths and weaknesses. The issues with this method are fairly clear – how well do pupils really know their character, and are all pupils likely to report honestly on themselves? It is for this reason that although self-reporting scales might provide an interesting picture, any findings from them should be treated with caution by schools.

Although there are other methods available, they too suffer from validity claims and also would be beyond the scope of most schools and teachers to implement effectively. The general rule is the more sophisticated the measure the harder it will be for schools to implement without buying in additional expertise. Moral dilemma tests (see, for example Thoma, 2006) are becoming more widespread but analysing and understanding the results is likely to present challenges to most teachers. Other types of measurement such as implicit testing and even brain scanning are in development – but these would certainly be beyond the scope of a primary school.

Some final considerations for schools seeking to measure character

The discussion above presents some of the challenges of measuring character. The question a primary school would need to ask is if they want to direct time and resources away from other school priorities to tackle the measurement problem. If they are seeking ways to measure character the following advice is intended to be helpful.

- Identify a member of staff to lead on character education evaluation for the school. This person should become aware of the challenges and limitations of measuring character, but also conduct research to gather up the tools and scales that are readily available. They can be in charge of developing the school's principles of measurement and developing a strategy that adheres to these principles.

- Most schools will rely on self-report measures. These can be made more robust by triangulating a pupil's reporting of their own character with how their peers, teachers and also perhaps parents rate their character strengths and weaknesses. The more data that can be brought into play the more accurate the picture is likely to be. For example the Character Growth Card, developed by Character Lab, combines evidence from pupils and teachers. The growth card has also been developed as an App (see https://characterlab.org/character-growth-card).

- Draw as much as possible on what is already available – as the hard work in development, piloting and validation of tools will have already been done. There are many commercially as well as freely available measurement tools – many of which can be downloaded from the internet. However, before attempting to use one of these tools think about how you are going to collect, collate and analyse the data, as this can be a big job and might require particular expertise. Also, always use caution when analysing results, given the challenges of accurately measuring character.

- If you are keen to test particular character education interventions it might only be necessary to evaluate what works through a pilot run in one or two 'experimental' classes rather than a whole school. Based on the findings the intervention can then be rolled out to the whole school if successful.

- Sign up to free character education newsletters – such as those produced by the Jubilee Centre, ACE and Character.org – as these often contain information about measuring character. Advice can also be gained from the Education Endowment Foundation, Character Lab and other organisations interested in this area.

Chapter summary

This chapter has looked at what might be the most suitable theoretical underpinnings of character education. It explains that most of the approaches to character education covered in the book are based on an interpretation of Aristotelian virtue ethics. Virtue ethics provides educationalists with tools including *eudaimonia* (happiness or flourishing), *arete* (excellence or virtue) and *phronesis* (practical or moral wisdom) that educational interventions can be built upon. The recent contributions of psychology and, in particular, the sub-discipline of positive psychology were discussed. The chapter closed by championing recent initiatives in cross-disciplinary approaches which have the potential to bear many useful fruits for teachers seeking strategies, tools, methods and resources based on academic research to use in the classroom.

Further reading

Kristjánsson, K. (2015) *Aristotelian Character Education.* Abingdon: Routledge.

One of the best books in the field arguing why character education should be essentially based on an Aristotelian conception of virtue ethics. The book explores the philosophy, as well as providing useful chapters on measuring virtue, the myths of character education, phronesis and educating the educators.

Morris, I. (2015) *Teaching Happiness and Well-being in Schools: Learning to ride elephants* (2nd edn). London: Bloomsbury.

This book explains how Aristotelian virtue theory can be used to create a philosophy of education, a whole-school practice of character education and it also explains the theoretical underpinnings of a well-being or character education curriculum, with ideas for how these concepts might be taught.

White, M. and Murray, S. (eds) (2015) *Evidence-Based Approaches in Positive Education.* New York and London: Springer.

The book, largely based on action research in schools, looks at how positive educational strategies designed to build character might be implemented at classroom and whole-school levels. The book highlights several evidence-based approaches to positive education that are useful for other teachers seeking inspiration for similar interventions they are keen to develop and try out.

References

Annas, J. (2011) *Intelligent Virtue*. Oxford: Oxford University Press.

Anscombe, G. E. M. (1958) Modern moral philosophy. *Philosophy*, 33 (124): 1–19.

Aristotle (1976) *Ethics* (translated by A. K. Thomson). Harmondsworth: Penguin.

Arthur, J. (2003) *Education with Character: The moral economy of schooling*. London: RoutledgeFalmer.

Arthur, J. and Harrison, T. (2012) Exploring good character and citizenship in England. *Asia Pacific Journal of Education,* 32 (4): 489–97.

Arthur, J., Harrison, T., Carr, D., Kristjánsson, K., and Davison, I. (2014) *Knightly Virtues: Enhancing Virtue Literacy Through Stories, Research Report.* Birmingham: University of Birmingham, Jubilee Centre for Character and Virtues. Available from: www.jubileecentre. ac.uk/1545/projects/development-projects/knightly-virtues (accessed 26 November 2014).

Badhwar, N.S. (1996) The limited unity of virtue. *Nous*, 30 (3): 306–29.

Bercowitz, M. and Bier, M. (2014) Research based fundamentals of the effective promotion of character development in schools. In Nucci, L., Narváez, D. and Krettenauer, T. (eds) *Handbook of Moral and Character Education* (2nd edn). New York and London: Routledge.

Benninga, J. S., Berkowitz, M. W., Kuehn, P. and Smith, K. (2003) The relationship of character education implementation and academic achievement in elementary schools. *Journal of Research in Character Education*, 1 (1): 19–32.

Blasi, A. (1980) Bridging moral cognition and moral action: a critical review of the literature'. *Psychological Bulletin*, 88, (1): 1–45.

Burden, R. (2014) *Myself as a Learner Scale*. Birmingham: Imaginative Minds.

Carr, D. (ed.) (2016) *Perspectives on Gratitude: An interdisciplinary approach*. London and New York: Routledge.

Dweck, C. (2008) *Mindset: How you can fulfill your potential*. New York: Random House.

Darwell, S. (ed.) (2003) *Virtue Ethics*. Oxford: Blackwells.

David, S. A., Boniwell, I. and Ayers, A. (2013) *The Oxford Handbook of Happiness*. Oxford: Oxford University Press.

Duckworth, A. and Peterson, C. (2007) Grit: Perseverance and passion for long-term goals. *Journal of Personality and Social Psychology*, 92 (6): 1087–101.

Hursthouse, R. (1999) *On Virtue Ethics*. Oxford: Oxford University Press.

Kristjánsson, K. (2015) *Aristotelian Character Education*. Abingdon: Routledge.

Kohlberg, L. (1973) A cognitive-developmental approach to moral education. In Kohlberg, L. (ed.) *Collected Papers on Moral Development and Moral Education*. Cambridge, MA: Center for Moral Education, Harvard University. pp. 13–16.

MacIntyre, A. (1981) *After Virtue*. London: Duckworth.

Madden, M., Lenhart, A., Cortesi, S. A., Gasser, U., Duggan, M., Smith, A. and Beaton, M. (2013) *Teens, Social Media and Privacy*. Washington, DC: Pew Research Centre.

McMahon, D. (2006) *The Pursuit of Happiness: A history from the Greeks to the present*. New York: Allen Lane.

Morris, I. (2015): *Teaching Happiness and Wellbeing in Schools: Learning to ride elephants* (2nd edn). London: Bloomsbury.

Narváez, D., Getz, I., Rest, J. R. and Thoma, S. (1999) Individual moral judgment and cultural ideologies. *Developmental Psychology*, 35: 478–88.

Noel, J. (1999) On the varieties of phronesis. *Educational Philosophy and Theory*, 31 (3): 273–89.

Nucci, L. P., Narváez, D. and Krettenauer, T. (eds) (2014) *The Handbook of Moral and Character Education* (2nd edn). New York and London: Routledge.

Peterson, C. and Seligman, M. E. P. (2004) *Character Strengths and Virtues: A handbook and classification*. Oxford: Oxford University Press.

Peterson, C. (2006) *A Primer in Positive Psychology*. New York: Oxford University Press.

Rae, T and MacConville, R (2015) *Using Positive Psychology to Enhance Student Achievement*. Abingdon: Routledge,

Rest, J. (1986) *Moral Development: Advances in Research and Theory*. New York: Praeger.

Sandel, M. (2010) *Justice*. London: Penguin Group.

Seligman, M. and Csikszentmihalyi, M. (2000) Positive psychology – an introduction. *American Psychologist*, 55 (1): 5–14.

Seligman, M., Ernst, R., Gillham, J., Reivich, K. and Linkins, M. (2009) Positive Education: Positive psychology and classroom interventions. *Oxford Review of Education*, 35: 293–311.

Seligman, M. (2011) *Flourish*. New York: Simon and Schuster.

Thoma, S. (2006) Research on defining issues test. In Killen, M. and Smetana, J. G. (eds) *Handbook of Moral Development*. Mahwah, NJ: Erlbaum.

Walker, D., Roberts, M. and Kristjánsson, K. (2015) Towards a new era of character education in theory and in practice. *Educational Review,* 67 (1): 79–96.

White, M. A. and Murray, S. (eds) (2014) *Evidence-Based Approaches in Positive Education*. New York and London: Springer.

White, M. and Waters, L. (2014) A case study of a good school: Example of the use of Peterson's strengths based approach with students. *The Journal of Positive Psychology*, 10 (1): 69–76.

4 Character education: taught and caught

In this chapter you will:

- gain a deeper understanding of the character caught/character taught debate;
- learn how to make character education intentional and an explicit part of your teaching;
- discover what the difference is between 'genuine' character education and more 'superficial' character education;
- understand the difference between learning *about* being virtuous and actually *becoming* more virtuous.

Introduction

Try to imagine a school where no character development happens amongst the children; where they make no progress morally or intellectually and acquire no performance or civic virtue. It's impossible isn't it? Not only that, but it's disturbing to think that a child could have such close contact with a school for so long and emerge with no meaningful growth in virtue or character at the end. Worse still, imagine a school which only contributes to the acquisition of vice; where the character formation is so negligent that the children complete their schooling worse off than when they began. It is exactly this kind of educational dystopia that Charles Dickens envisaged in Gradgrind's school in *Hard Times*, where children are bullied through an instrumental, knowledge-only curriculum and wind up either emotionally traumatised, or so short on empathy that they are monstrous.

This thought experiment reminds us that character development – for good or ill – is an inevitable outcome of schooling. It also helps to reveal that we feel some kind of imperative within us as educators to contribute positively and meaningfully to the moral, intellectual, civic and performance virtues of the children we teach, because the suggestion that it might be absent is troubling. In the light of the four domains of virtue (see Chapter 2), it also becomes clear that character education and schooling are inseparable; that one of the main purposes of education – if not *the* main purpose – is the development of good character with the superior aim of helping to bring about the flourishing and well-being of young people.

The death knell sounding in the background to the character education debate is the phrase 'we do this anyway'. This phrase suggests not only an unwillingness to accommodate new ideas, but also an unwillingness to make our teaching practice more deliberate and sophisticated. Aristotle tells us that *'playing the harp makes both good and bad harpists'*. In the same way that playing a musical instrument depends upon an understanding of music theory and practising the instrument with the aim of improving and refining our technique, so too teaching – and teaching character – depends upon an understanding of the pedagogy and the theory, as well as the well-intentioned practice of teaching to the virtues in a variety of ways, across the four domains of virtue. It is very easy to acknowledge that our existing practice and the ethos of our school *in some vague way* already contributes towards the development of good character, but it is *virtuous practice* to want to teach character in a deliberate and skilful way (see Annas, 2011). Arguing that character education is a mysterious process that 'just sort of happens', as if by accident, leaves too much to chance. As James Arthur (2003, p.118) suggests, it may well be that the so-called 'hidden curriculum' of a school (its culture, ethos and values) has a more powerful impact on pupil behaviour than the taught curriculum. If this is true, school communities have a duty to reflect critically upon the hidden curriculum and its impact so that it is hidden no longer; if anything, to avoid the hidden curriculum being one that is harmful. To say 'we do this anyway' is to acquiesce to a second-best state of affairs which abdicates us as educational professionals from our responsibility to refine and improve our practice. If we acknowledge our duty to teach character, we should similarly acknowledge our duty to do so consciously and deliberately.

So how do we do it consciously and deliberately? This raises a well-rehearsed question about whether character education is *caught* by creating a school ethos which promotes the development of good character, or whether it is *taught* through a curriculum constructed with the intention of educating for character. It is the aim of this chapter to begin to demonstrate that this is in fact a false dichotomy: that it's not a question of either/or, but instead a question of how *both* can be used to mutual benefit.

What does it mean for character to be caught?

[C]haracter education is rarely formally recorded in any lesson plans or schemes of work – rather it forms part of the hidden curriculum. No primary teacher in Britain would doubt how the school often acts as a family for many pupils, replicating some of the formative influences of the family environment – warmth, acceptance, caring relationships, love and positive role models.

(Arthur, 2003, p. 118)

From the very first moment a child lets go of her parent's hand and makes her way into a classroom, she embarks upon a journey of monumental personal change. The community she now finds herself in will make demands on her that are new and on a scale that may be fascinating and daunting. Her job is to try to make sense of this new environment and what is expected of her and she will do this by paying very close attention to the elements of this community that she believes will help her to understand it. She will be looking for patterns and asking herself 'what is it that people regularly do in this place and how can I emulate these behaviours so that I can fit in?' The ethos of a school is made up of how people habitually interact with each other, from the basics of how we greet and show gratitude, to the systems and structures that support learning, relationships, activities, the arts, service and caring.

In *Education with Character*, James Arthur (2003, p.118) cites Edward Wynne's observation that schools can teach morality, through the ethos, without saying a single word about it. If a school accepts that its ethos will unavoidably have an impact on the character formation of the children – and adults – who pass through its care, this places an onus of responsibility upon that community to deliberately and carefully examine how the ethos of the school affects the way in which virtue is caught by its members. As Ron Berger suggests, the development of an ethos which fosters good character is not easy:

> *Building and maintaining a positive community takes constant vigilance. Like raising young children, it's a job that's never really done. Frequently it's discouraging and overwhelming. To have a quality school, however, I don't think there's any choice – it takes attention always, and lots of it.*
>
> (Berger, 2003, p.50)

Because a school ethos is built upon relationships which are dynamic and constantly shifting, our efforts to produce the kind of ethos and relationships which result in schools that positively impact upon character must be continuous. A school's moral climate requires careful thought and attention alongside high expectations and the knowledge that, when people are unkind, unfair or disrespectful, this will not go ignored and unaddressed. Of course, some children will walk into a new school community having taken different developmental steps to others, which makes the task of schools in creating an ethos of virtue development more salient. This point is emphasised here by Kristjan Kristjansson:

> [C]hildren who have not been brought up in good habits need to be exposed to the sort of transformative forces that can make radical self-change, through the contemplative route, possible. More specifically they need to be exposed to teachers who can act as moral exemplars.
>
> (Kristjánsson, 2015, p.116)

As we will see in Part 3, a significant contributor to school ethos is the acknowledgement by teachers that their role goes beyond 'delivering' a curriculum. Because children shape their moral virtues in no small part through observing the conduct of adults, the adults in a learning community must work hard on a daily basis to role-model virtues in action. For Nel Noddings, a moral climate can only be fostered if teachers see themselves as the 'one-caring':

> *The one-caring as teacher, then, has two major tasks: to stretch the student's world by presenting an effective selection of that world with which she is in contact, and to work cooperatively with the student in his struggle toward competence in that world. But her task as one-caring has higher priority than either of these. First and foremost she must nurture the child's ethical ideal.*
>
> (Noddings, 1986, p.178)

For Noddings, Arthur and Berger, the conundrum of how to orientate the school ethos so that it helps form good character for all members of the community is resolved through having a clear and shared common purpose, built upon caring and respectful relationships. For all three, the emphasis is upon widening children's moral and intellectual horizons: challenging and enabling them to reason and think through new concepts and supporting them to refine their emotional responses to the circumstances of their lives. Where teachers feel that they are collaborating with colleagues on these projects and where all exert the kind of vigilance that Berger writes about, a school ethos stands a good chance of fostering good character. This is not to advocate an educational environment which consists of blind adherence to centrally dictated policies or conformity to a one-size-fits-all, tick box, technocratic approach to teaching. Character education cannot be imposed from the top down. What is striking about Berger's reflections on his experience of helping to shape the school where he teaches is the underlying theme of struggle, disagreement and intense dialogue with colleagues. A common purpose can only have a chance of lasting if teachers (and children) believe that they participate in its formation and are also given a degree of autonomy and professional respect in how they make their unique contribution to it. From time to time, this will lead to conflict, out of which something better may have a chance of emerging.

There are also red herrings when it comes to ethos: side-shows which purport to form good character, but which in practice may just be ignored or at worst have an underlying message of promoting conformity. One could be forgiven for believing that if we bombard children with messages about ethos in the form of posters, slogans, mottoes, vast murals and lists of 'our values' and 'our behaviours', that via some mystical process of osmosis the children will become more morally sophisticated. They won't. They will just learn to parrot what they see, instead of developing reasoned motivations for doing the good. One of the clear messages to emerge from the writing about Aristotelian approaches to character education is that there are no quick fixes to making people moral agents, and that the learning takes place in the context of relationships, not by simply looking at the posters which illuminate whichever virtues the school happens to have chosen.

What does it mean for character to be taught?

> [C]haracter education is continuous with everyday teaching, and not an extra task that is essentially unrelated to the transfer of subject-related knowledge and skills... When schools take the moral dimension of teaching very seriously, 'character education' can become an encompassing theme included in the curriculum, staff meetings and teacher training and thus embedded in a school's culture.
>
> (Sanderse, 2012, pp.123–4)

Part 2 will go into detail about the mechanics of a taught course in character education, both as a discrete subject and as an approach to teaching the (national) curriculum. As a prelude, it is worth considering why, if a school ethos can be constructed which successfully teaches character without directly mentioning it, we should go to the effort of constructing discrete lessons, or shaping existing curriculum content to bring about character educational aims.

In *Intelligent Virtue*, Julia Annas likens the acquisition of a virtue to the acquisition of a skill and she suggests that this is driven along by two elements, the *need to learn* and *the drive to aspire*. For Annas, it is not possible to truly acquire a virtue unless we understand what that virtue is through learning about it from a role model:

> The learner needs to understand what in the role model to follow, what the point is of doing something this way rather than that, what is crucial to the teacher's way of doing things and what is not... Finally, aspiration leads the learner to strive to improve, to do what he is doing better rather than taking it over by rote from the teacher.
>
> (Annas, 2011, pp.17–18)

In thinking about how we might go about the deliberate teaching of virtue and character, there is an important distinction to be made between *learning about virtue* and *learning to be virtuous*. As Aristotle points out in *The Nicomachean Ethics*, 'we are inquiring not in order to know what virtue is, but in order to become good'. It is tempting to think that knowledge of virtue – either in the form of knowing virtue words and vocabulary, or knowing virtue stories from literature – is enough to guide action. It is not: just ask the thousands of people who take up smoking each year in the full knowledge that it is life-limiting. This is not to say that virtue knowledge doesn't matter, but we need to be cautious about the capacity of knowledge alone to guide action.

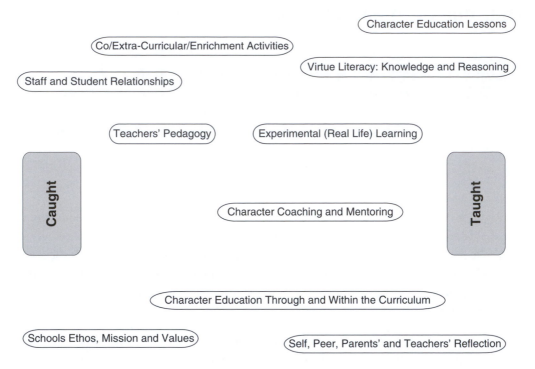

Figure 4.1 Caught and taught

Virtue caught and taught

James Arthur (2003, p.115) cites the work of Kevin Ryan and Thomas Lickona, who suggest a model of character development based on three elements: knowledge, affect and action. Growth in virtue, through a need to learn, depends upon *knowledge* of the virtues, awareness of the *emotional* component of using the virtues and an understanding of how *my will and my habits* affect my actions. It can be hoped that these issues will be addressed through the school ethos, but it is not entirely clear how this could happen in the absence of deliberate teaching. In order to develop knowledge and understanding of virtue and also to reflect on how this knowledge and understanding is having an impact upon me, I will need time with a skilled mentor. A mentor who can help me to deepen my understanding and inspire me to want to keep improving, through helping me to develop a language and cognitive framework of virtue to make sense of my experiences. This can only really be provided by some form of deliberate and well-designed curriculum, which forms one part of a whole-school ethos of caring relationships. In this sense, curriculum and ethos can work hand in hand to produce ever more sophisticated understanding, feeling and action: character education has to be both caught and taught.

Further reading

Seider, S. (2012) *Character Compass: How powerful school culture can point students towards success.* Cambridge, MA: Harvard Education Press.

This book offers portraits of three high-performing urban schools in Boston, Massachusetts, that have made character development central to their mission of supporting student success, yet define character in three very different ways. One school focuses on students' moral character development, another emphasises civic character development, and the third prioritises performance character development. Drawing on surveys, interviews, field notes and student achievement data, *Character Compass* highlights the unique effects of these distinct approaches to character development as well as the implications for parents, educators, and policymakers committed to fostering powerful school culture in their own school communities.

References

Annas, J. (2011) *Intelligent Virtue*. Oxford: Oxford University Press.

Arthur, J. (2003) *Education with Character: The moral economy of schooling*. London: RoutledgeFalmer.

Berger, R. (2003) *An Ethic of Excellence.* Portsmouth, NH: Heinemann.

Kristjánsson, K. (2015) *Aristotelian Character Education*. London: Routledge.

Noddings, N. (1986) *Caring: A Relational Approach to Ethics and Moral Education.* Berkley, CA: University of California Press.

Sanderse, W. (2012) *Character Education: A neo-Aristotelian approach to the philosophy, psychology and education of virtue.* Delft: Eburon.

Part 2

Character education – taught

Part 1 made the case that character can be taught and caught. Part 2 explores approaches and strategies for 'teaching character' in primary schools. This part is split into three chapters. Chapter 5 describes what a discrete taught course in character education might encompass and how this relates to other subjects such as PSHE and citizenship. Chapter 6 explains how character can be educated through and within other subjects such as English, maths, science and PE. Both these chapters provide practical advice and lesson ideas for ensuring that character education is a visible and conscious part of primary schooling. Part 2 closes with some consideration of how taught approaches to character education might be assessed and pupil progress evaluated.

5 A taught course in character education

In this chapter you will:

- learn how to structure a character education curriculum;
- understand the difference between virtue knowledge, virtue reasoning and virtue practice;
- discover the caterpillar process for developing virtue;
- view an example series of lessons on fairness for Reception to Year 6 pupils.

Introduction

This chapter moves swiftly from the theory of character education to its practice. The aim of the chapter is to demonstrate to readers the value of a taught course in character education. As previously explained, a taught course ensures that a primary school's character education curriculum is intentional and planned. Lessons in various aspects of character also ensure that pupils develop a language of character as well as being provided with some tools to reflect on how they might build their own characters. The chapter details some of the steps teachers need to go through in order to plan and develop a taught course – this includes a consideration of how best to structure the curriculum. An explanation of virtue knowledge, virtue reasoning and virtue practice is provided – as these should all form central pillars of any taught course. The caterpillar process is also explained as one approach that might be adopted to help teachers and pupils identify the main steps of becoming virtuous. At the end of the chapter a series of lessons on fairness, drawn from the Jubilee Centre primary programme of study are included. The lessons are provided as a model for teachers to use when developing their own curriculum materials.

Structuring a character education curriculum

As we have seen in previous chapters, character is broadly made up of the acquisition of virtue across four domains: moral, intellectual, performance and civic. A complete curriculum aiming to address character education will place a direct emphasis on each of these areas. In many respects, the academic curriculum comprising literacy, numeracy, science, languages, humanities and the arts will take care of the intellectual virtues, although some attention may need to be given to illuminating specific intellectual virtues which enable us to access the curriculum, such as memory, comparison, description and explanation.

The moral, performance and civic virtues can enhance and enrich the teaching of the academic curriculum because of the opportunities they provide for understanding academic learning in its relational (moral), social (civic) and performance contexts. Human learning takes place within relationships, either to the teacher, to other learners or to the thing learned about. In order to do this fully, we need to develop moral skill. We also need to place learning in its civic context as more sophisticated understanding of the world can enable us to transform societies at the global and local level. Academic learning also depends upon meta-cognitive skills of learning about learning: the performance virtues such as the ability to persist with learning that is difficult or which requires attention over a long period of time.

A character-focused curriculum can also be used to encompass and develop existing requirements to teach PSHE (Personal, Social, Health and Economic education) material as in many respects these contain themes which speak directly to the acquisition of virtue. Primary schools in the UK are free to develop their own approaches to the teaching of PSHE, and character and virtue could be a vehicle for transforming it into learning about how to make wise choices and live a good, full human life. For example, the UK Department for Education guidance on PSHE (2015) suggests the teaching of 'diet for a healthy lifestyle'. When looked at through the prism of virtue, this can become a rich study of food knowledge, regulating our desires for fatty or sugary foods, the moral implications of harming our bodies through poor diet, and perhaps even the civic, citizenship issues of campaigning for things like clearer labelling of food packaging or ethical treatment of animals.

A curriculum aimed at the development of character should give weight to each of the four domains of virtue and it should do so in a way that enables children to acquire an explicit and clear understanding of the processes involved in acquiring virtue: virtue *knowledge*, virtue *reasoning* and virtue *practice*.

Virtue knowledge, virtue reasoning, virtue practice

Before the work of populating each lesson with content and each key stage with lessons begins, it's important to have some guiding, structural principles and concepts that give coherence to the overall curriculum that the children experience. This matters for two reasons. Firstly, it avoids contradictory messages within the learning and ensures that good work isn't undone later. Secondly, it enables teachers to build upwards on very solid foundations of learning, constantly reinforcing the concepts with ever more detailed and complex teaching as time goes on.

Perhaps chief amongst these concepts and principles is the precise nature of the way that virtue is learned. This is made up of three interrelated and mutually supporting aspects: virtue knowledge, virtue reasoning and virtue practice, which can be turned into a process, known as the caterpillar process (which is explained below).

Moral virtue involves the ability to educate our emotional responses to situations using reason. The virtue of courage for example, enables us to regulate the emotion of fear, which in turn enables us to avoid the vices of cowardice (where we succumb to fear) and foolhardiness (where we do not heed the message of fear to exercise caution). Virtue knowledge depends upon being able to do the following things.

1. Recognise and name particular virtues.

2. Recognise and name situations which call for those particular virtues by...

3. ... recognising the emotions we and others feel in particular situations.

4. Observing what it is that people who have developed the virtue can do particularly well.

When constructing a character education curriculum, virtue knowledge is one of the principal strands that need to be developed. Children need to be given an opportunity to recognise the virtues and the emotions which they regulate and they also need to be given an opportunity to learn from those who display the virtue. Role models do not necessarily have to be great heroes of virtue: some of the most powerful learning takes place when we see our peers doing something particularly well and we are then motivated to emulate their example.

A good way of building virtue knowledge is through the use of story. For example, Dr Seuss's story *The Lorax* has two main characters who clearly display certain virtues and vices. Providing children with some virtue and vice words (courage, care, respect, greed, selfishness, ignorance) and then reading the story together helps children build their virtue vocabulary, and also helps them to see what virtues and vices look like in action. Another writer who can be used in this way is Roald Dahl, whose characters tend to have their virtues and vices nicely exaggerated to make them easy to identify, but who also face some difficult moral decisions which draw upon virtue for their resolution: such as Danny's decision to illegally drive a car to help his father in *Danny the Champion of the World*, or Mr Fox's decision to burgle to feed his family in *Fantastic Mr Fox*.

Learning virtue depends upon a level of knowledge of virtue itself which can then, once we realise that we are deficient in the virtue, lead to the motivation to want to get better.

Virtue knowledge is not enough to be virtuous: the knowledge needs to be put into action – which is where virtue reasoning comes in. Virtue reasoning involves the following things.

1. Appreciating why a particular virtue is good by understanding how it benefits individuals and communities.

2. Understanding the '*middle-way*': doing the right thing, at the right time, in the right way, towards the right person and for the right reasons; understanding that there are middle ways of feeling and acting in any situation and that these middle ways are the virtue.

3. Giving (our own) and taking (from others) good reasons for our actions.

4. Developing awareness of how we typically act in certain situations and making decisions about what habits we might need to change.

Virtue reasoning not only depends upon virtue knowledge, but also enriches it. It takes those building blocks of knowledge and applies them to awareness of our inner world and our own moral development, and an awareness of our social world and our impact upon it. Coming to greater appreciation of how we reason in situations requiring virtue can also result in the realisation that we need to deepen our virtue knowledge by, for example, finding out how others have deployed a particular virtue that we now realise we lack.

Virtue practice takes the elements of knowledge and reasoning and helps a person to incorporate them into their sense of self through actually practising the virtues and reflecting on the impact that this practice has on us. It is made up of the following elements.

1. Putting the virtue(s) into action.

2. Observing and learning from others who put the virtues into action.

3. The ability to reflect upon events that have happened, to learn from them and to grow in understanding of how to act well.

4. Consciously and deliberately forming habits of virtuous action, with awareness of the person we are becoming.

It is with this third element of character education that we see learning about virtue take a stride beyond the classroom. There are obvious opportunities within a primary classroom for reinforcing what virtuous action would look like, but true virtue happens in the absence of a teacher or mentor where a person is intrinsically motivated and skilful enough to do the right thing at the right time. The ultimate and long-term aim of character education is for individuals to move beyond teachers, rules, rewards and sanctions: that they can decide well for themselves; that they are morally autonomous. Virtue practice is concerned with enabling children to recognise episodes in their lives where virtue is required, to draw upon virtue knowledge and reasoning to act deliberately and then to reflect on what happened in order to learn for next time.

Reflection is not an innate human capacity, as it relies upon cognitive structures in the brain which take time to develop and may not be complete until early adulthood. However, research into neuro-plasticity indicates that the brain is shaped by the experiences we feed it with (Doidge, 2008; Ratey, 2003). The more that we provide children with a supportive environment where they can think back over recent events, examine what they were thinking and feeling and ask how they might act differently in the future, the greater the chance of them developing a sophisticated reflective capacity over time. It is this upon which virtue hinges.

Once all three of these elements are combined (knowledge, reasoning, practice) and developed over time, this will contribute to young people being competent and free in making sensible and wise (moral) choices in the situations they face. This is not a quick process and there will be stumbles, trips and falls along the way. But then, this can be just as true for us as adults as it is for the children we work with.

The caterpillar process: bringing knowledge, reasoning and practice to life

Of central importance to the success of character education, is the opportunity for children to develop an internal language and process of developing in virtue: one that is simple, clear and effective. The Jubilee Centre materials for character education describe a five-stage process called *the caterpillar process*, after Eric Carle's popular children's book *The Very Hungry Caterpillar*. The process has five stages, which square with knowledge, reasoning and practice, but which has the added benefit of being an image that might be easier to remember. The five stages are as follows.

1. **Stop.** This involves the ability to either pause before making a decision, or to pause afterwards to reflect upon decisions that we have taken. It is based upon the skills of emotional regulation that enable us to pause before leaping in to a situation.

2. **Notice.** This involves gathering more information about the situations in which we find ourselves and instead of just going with our first thoughts, finding out more in an attempt to see situations as they are, rather than as we would like them to be.

3. **Look.** This involves observing our own emotions and the emotions of others. The emotions give us information about what we perceive and what others perceive and they are not always appropriate. The *middle way* encourages us to feel the right things, at the right time, in the right way, towards the right people, for the right reasons.

4. **Listen.** This involves the giving and taking of reasons for the things that we decide to do and the feelings that we have. Aristotle encourages us to educate the emotions with reason and educate reason with emotion to slowly refine our responses. This stage also encourages us to listen to our knowledge of the virtues and apply it practically to situations.

5. **Caterpillar.** In *The Very Hungry Caterpillar*, the colours of the food the caterpillar eats end up on the wings of the butterfly he becomes. In the same way, what we think, feel, say and do end up 'colouring' the person that we are becoming. This final step involves reflecting upon how we have responded across the previous four stages, with a view to changing responses that are lacking in virtue.

This reflective process can be applied to any learning done across the four domains of virtue, as any form of learning involves pausing, gathering information, feeling, thinking and reflecting to improve future performance. In the early stages of understanding this process, time will need to be taken to deliberately develop each aspect. For example, 'pausing' can be developed using mindfulness techniques, and 'looking' will involve developing an understanding of how emotions manifest themselves in our body through feelings, facial expressions and posture. Very young children may not yet have learned how to identify and read these signals.

The language teachers use is a powerful tool to develop and shape character and to help pupils be aware of and make progress in their moral development. As such, teachers should consider the advice on character coaching outlined in Chapter 11 before embarking on delivering any taught course in character education.

A taught course

The main challenges in devising a taught programme of character education are first, making sure that what is taught is directly relevant to the children at the stage of development they find themselves in, so that they can connect what they are learning to their own experience. This may seem like a statement of the obvious, but it's surprising how often this seems to be forgotten. Second, the learning should use particular issues to develop an understanding of how virtue is acquired over time through knowledge, reasoning and practice. There are ideas for how we might go about assessing for this learning in Chapter 7.

One approach to this can be found in the programme of study for primary years character education developed by experienced primary teachers for the Jubilee Centre for Character and Virtue (Jubilee Centre, 2015).

The programme of study teaches directly to 17 different virtues from the moral, civic and performance domains over the course of a single school year. The course is structured so that a whole school community is focusing on a single virtue at a time and that as children proceed up through the school years, each virtue will be revisited each year so that understanding of those virtues develops and deepens. This has the added benefit of creating opportunities for children across year groups to work together to share their learning about how a particular virtue can be practically applied to their own experience. The programme of study introduces each virtue through the kinds of situations where children might find themselves needing to use it. For example, courage is first encountered in the autumn term of Reception where

Autumn	Spring	Summer
Caring	Cleanliness	Courtesy
Helpfulness	Fairness	Forgiveness
Cooperation	Friendliness	Determination
Courage	Service	Self-discipline
Kindness	Patience	Gratitude
	Respect	Honesty

Table 5.1 Teaching 17 virtues across the school year

children look at 'trying new things'; their peers in Year 3 will be looking at how courage can help them to learn from mistakes; and in Year 5, they are exploring how to face their fears. The table below shows when each virtue is approached.

As James Arthur (2003) points out, it is for schools to determine for themselves what is most salient for their communities. The 17 virtues set out in the Jubilee Centre programme of study should by no means be seen as an exclusive or perfect list and it is for schools to work out which virtues they focus on, rather than slavishly work their way through a folder of materials. What is of greater importance is that children learn about the process of acquiring and developing virtue, and also that they acquire a vocabulary and knowledge of virtue which helps them to make sense of their experiences and slowly learn to take more responsibility for their growth in character. Below are some sample lesson plans from the Jubilee Centre materials for Reception through to Year 6, for the virtue of fairness/justice.

Reception	'It's not fair'
	Intro: 'Have you ever said, "It's not fair"? I think that everyone in this room may have said or at least thought those words. Can you think of a time when you have said this or when you might say this? Today we are going to think about how we feel when we think that something is not fair.'
	1. Sit the children around in a circle and open up the bag of sweets/biscuits. Now, hand out the treats to one group of children only e.g. boys/girls/blonde hair/birthdays in October etc. Tell the children that they are allowed to eat their treats. Now explain to the children your reason for giving the treats to that particular group, e.g. they are boys etc.
	2. Ask each child to hold up an emotions card to show how they feel about this. Ask some of the children to explain why they chose that particular emotion. Ask the children whether or not your actions were fair and why. Now ask the children how this could be made fair – explore the options of giving every child a treat or a valid reason for giving certain children a treat, e.g. exceptional behaviour/kindness.
	3. Now give treats to the remaining children and ask everyone to show their emotions cards again. Ask for feedback about the selections from some children. Now ask the children who chose different emotions to try and explain in words how they felt before and how they feel now.
Year 1	Fair shares for others
	Lesson 1
	Intro: 'There are many things that are happening around us and around the world every day that are unfair in different ways. Sometimes it can be tricky to decide whether something is fair if it is not happening to us. Today, you will decide whether what you see is fair or not.'
	Suggested resources: Photographs of different situations on a PowerPoint (you may want to print these off as an additional resource). 'Fair' and 'unfair' labels for continuum.
	1. Put up the 'fair' and 'unfair' signs at opposite ends of the classroom and explain to the children that you will show them some images.
	2. Go on to explain that they will need to decide whether the picture is fair or unfair and show their decision by moving to the appropriate end of the classroom. Tell the children that they must not just follow their friends but make a decision for themselves as you will be asking them why they made their choices.

⟶

	3. Carry out the activity, asking children why they chose as they did – give children the opportunity to change their minds and move if their peers give explanations that make them think differently.
	4. Hand out 'fair' and 'unfair' blank sheets and ask the children to draw a picture of something they think is fair and something they think is unfair.
	Lesson 2
	Intro: 'In the last lesson, we looked at some pictures of fairness and unfairness. In some of the pictures, we saw people who live very different lives to ourselves. We are very lucky that we have food on the table each day, warm homes to sleep in at night, fresh water available whenever we need it and much more. Some people have very little. Is this fair? Because we are so lucky to have these things, we must make sure that we do not take it for granted or waste what we have.'
	Suggested resources: WaterAid 'water around the world' PowerPoint (available from: http://www.wateraid. org/uk/get-involved/schools/primary-resources), colouring pens/pencils, poster templates. (sample available from: http://www.nrcan.gc.ca/sites/www.nrcan.gc.ca/files/kidsclub/colouring-page-brushing-2.jpg.
	1. Show children the WaterAid PowerPoint – discuss some of the images and important facts with them.
	2. Ask them if they think that the children in the picture have a fair share of the world's water. Discuss the responses and draw comparisons to the way that we use and access water ourselves.
	3. Explore the question of how many times children use water every day and what they use it for. Talk to the children about what they do when they brush their teeth – do they turn off the tap when they are brushing or do they sometimes leave it running?
	4. Ask the children to explain the importance of being responsible and saving water where we can. Tell the children that today they are going to make posters that will be laminated and that they can take home to remind people to turn off the taps and save water. (If taps at school do not automatically shut off, you may want to display some posters around school.)
Year 2	**Fairness and food**
	Intro: 'Today children we are going to think about ourselves as part of the world. We are going to talk about fairness and ask the question "Is our world fair?" You will work as a class to decide whether you think it is or not and, if you decide it is not, what we can do to try to change that.'
	Suggested resources: Global Mindshift 'Wombat' video (https://youtu.be/GqJUeRltxs8 (available 10/15). 100 small sweets.
	1. Divide the children up into four groups: one large group (approximately half of the class); two small groups (about seven children in each); and two children in the final group. These numbers can be altered, as can the number of groups; the idea is that the children gain an understanding about the inequality of world food distribution.
	2. Tell the children that you have 100 sweets. Ask them to work in their groups to decide how many sweets they think their group should get and why and also how many sweets the other groups should get and why.
	3. Give the children some time to discuss this and then ask them to feed back. The children will most probably draw on the idea of fairness and this will be reflected in the amount of sweets that they have allocated to each group.
	4. Tell them that you have decided how many you are going to give to each group – as you give them out, count out loud so that the children know how many each group have been given. Give the large group about 10 sweets, the two middle groups about 20 each and then the remaining 50 to the group of two children. Feed off the responses from the children. What do they think about this? Why is this not fair?

	5. Ask the children to imagine that they are a country – which country might they be? The two children should be told that they represent the UK – what could they do now to make things more fair? Hopefully, the children will consider giving some of their food to the other countries, particularly the largest group.
Year 3	**Two sides to every story**
	Intro: 'Today we are going to be learning about how important it is to not make snap judgements about people or situations. We need to make sure we understand that sometimes we only hear one side of a story and that it would be unfair for us to make a judgement or give an opinion without having all of the facts.'
	Suggested resources: https://youtu.be/m75aEhm-BYw (available 10/15), 'Wolf' character profile sheets.
	1. Ask the children to recall the story of The Three Little Pigs. What are the main parts of the story? Storyboard these on the whiteboard for children to see.
	2. Now ask the children to work in pairs to play 'One Word at a Time' – the children retell the story between them but they are only allowed to say one word at a time. This should enable the children to familiarise themselves with the characters and main events.
	3. Take the character of the Big Bad Wolf and ask the children 'Who thinks the wolf is a bad character?' (children should raise their hands to show their response – count the number for later).
	4. Now, ask them to describe the wolf's character, justifying their choices.
	5. Discuss the name given to the character and what this name makes us think as soon as we hear it, even before we have read the story.
	6. Now show children the video clip of the story from the wolf's point of view. Ask the children 'What was different about the story? Why was this different?'
	7. Hand out the wolf character profile sheets to each child and ask them to describe the wolf that they saw in the video, not the one from the original story. Ask the children to feed back some of their descriptive phrases/words.
	8. Conscience Alley – divide the class into two and ask them to stand in two lines facing each other to form an alley. Ask one side of the room to think about the wolf in the original story and the other to think about the wolf in the video that they saw. They must say aloud the descriptive phrases and adjectives they think describe the wolf as the children take it in turns to walk through the alley. Explain to the children that they need to listen carefully as they walk through the alley so that they can hear two points of view.
	9. Now ask again, 'Hands up if you think that the wolf is a bad character?' Count the number of hands raised and compare with the number at the start of the lesson. Ask one of the children who changed their mind why they did so. Highlight the objective again to pupils.
Year 4	**School rules**
	Intro: 'Today we are going to look at the reasons why we have rules and in particular why we have to have rules in school.'
	Suggested resources: http://donnayoung.org/homeschooling/games/game-boards.htm (available 10/15) (free printable board game templates – one between four or five pupils). Dice for each group of children. Counters for each child.
	1. Divide the class into groups of four or five children and give each group a blank game board, counters and a set of dice. Ask the children to play the game but do not give them any instructions or rules about how to play.
	2. The children will most likely be confused about what to do and start asking questions – try to encourage them to continue to try playing as best they can.
	3. After a few more minutes – ask the children to stop and ask them why they found the game difficult to play. Elicit from the children that it was complicated because they were not given any rules or instructions. Find out what the children did to enable them to start trying to play the game. Talk about the problems that arise when lots of different people make up rules – e.g. arguments, not knowing which rules to follow.

→

	4. Ask the children to think about and come up with reasons why rules might be important. 5. Hand out the school rules to the children (if you have them) and ask them to work in pairs to number the rules in terms of their importance – which do they think is the most important rule and why, and which is the least important and why? 6. Gather some feedback from the children and, as a class, see if they can agree on the most important rule. Now ask the children to work in groups to discuss each rule – why do we have this rule in school? What would happen if we did not have this as a school rule? Now ask the children if they agree with all of the rules. Are there any that they would change, or indeed are there any that they think need to be added and, if so, why? 7. Ask the children to create one new rule that they think should become part of the school rules. Explain to the children that these will then be passed on to the school council or proposed to the head teacher.
Year 5	**Point of view** Intro: 'Often, we look at pictures or situations and only see them from our own point of view – from the way that we are looking at something. Today, we are going to think about this in more detail – we will be thinking about why it might be good to see things from the point of view of others.' *Suggested resources*: http://pbskids.org/cyberchase/math-games/point-out-view/ (available 10/15); the story of The Blind Men and the Elephant (available on the internet along with images to show the children and illustrate the story), laptops/internet access, one between two children. 1. Children access the above link in pairs and play the game. This will be a good prompt for discussion about the fact that the children in the picture are all looking at the same blocks but the way that they see the blocks depends on the position that they are looking at it from. 2. Now read the story of The Blind Men and the Elephant – take in responses from the children. What do they learn from the story? Help the children to understand that this story can help us to think about the different views of people in life. For example, many believe that there is only one God, but people sometimes see this God in different ways and use different names for God. 3. Retell a well-known story/fairy tale to the children. Explain to the children that more often than not in these traditional stories, they are told from the perspective of the narrator. This is considered as a neutral position; the narrator does not usually have an opinion. 4. Now explain to the children that you want them to take on the role of one of the characters in the story and retell the same story from that particular character's point of view. Ask the children to repeat this task, taking on a new character. 5. Ask the children to work in pairs to think of a time when they have had an argument with someone else. Ask the children to tell their partners about the argument. Now ask the children to retell the story from the other person's point of view. If they had thought about this at the time, would the outcome have been different?
Year 6	**Justice** Intro: 'Today we will be exploring the meaning of justice. We will try to decide on a clear definition of the word and think about examples of justice in society today.' 1. Ask the children what they believe the word 'justice' means. Take in the suggestions and record these on the whiteboard. 2. Ask the children to find the dictionary definition of the word. 3. Now organise the children into groups of five or six and give them a large piece of sugar paper. Label half of the pieces of sugar paper with 'just' and the other half with 'unjust'. 4. Ask the children to work in groups to look through some news articles and find those that match with the heading on their paper.

	5. Each group to feed back the headlines that they have chosen and choose one of the stories to explain in more detail.
	6. Take an example of one of the newspaper stories. Unpick the story as a class and discuss whether there is evidence of justice in this story.
	7. Now explain to the children that they are going to write their own newspaper articles about something that has happened in school and that they must try to show how justice has been served.

Table 5.2 Sample lesson plans: fairness

Chapter summary

This chapter has focused on how character can be taught in primary schools. In particular it has considered creating a discrete space within the curriculum where the development of moral, civic, performance and intellectual virtues can be explicitly built (space which might otherwise be occupied by PSHE). The chapter started out with an explanation of how to structure a character education curriculum. It then provided an overview of the recommended pillars of any taught character education approach; namely, virtue knowledge, virtue reasoning and virtue practice. A particular technique for the enhancement of virtue practice, called the caterpillar process was explained. The chapter finished with an example series of lessons on fairness suitable for Reception to Year 6 pupils.

Further reading

Character Education Programme of Study – Primary Schools

Available at: http://jubileecentre.ac.uk/1635/character-education

The programme of study provides a taught course in character education for Reception to Year 6. The course is divided into three terms and separated into individual year groups. Each term's curriculum is divided into sequences of lessons which address particular virtues. The course allows flexibility to suit individual school/teacher approaches. Teacher's notes and accompanying PowerPoint presentations are also provided.

References

Annas, J. (2011) *Intelligent Virtue*. Oxford: Oxford University Press.

Doidge, N. (2008) *The Brain That Changes Itself*. London: Penguin.

Jubilee Centre (2015) Primary Programme of Study for Character Education. Birmingham: University of Birmingham. Available at:http://jubileecentre.ac.uk/1635/character-education (accessed 9 December 2015).

Ratey, J. (2003) *A User's Guide to the Brain*. London: Abacus.

6 Teaching character through the curriculum

In this chapter you will:

- understand how character can be taught through and within different subjects in the primary curriculum;
- gain an in-depth understanding of how to teach character through English – and in particular through stories;
- understand how to draw out the moral and emotional content of stories using The Lorax as an example;
- see the link between teaching English and the development of performance virtues including persistence and determination;
- learn how character education can be taught through and within ten other subjects – including maths and science.

Introduction

Chapter 5 examined how primary schools can go about constructing a discrete curriculum directly aimed at the teaching of character, the principal concerns of which are to develop *virtue knowledge*, *virtue reasoning* and *virtue practice*, as well as equipping children with an internalised process of the acquisition of virtue, brought to life through *the caterpillar process*. This addresses the idea of character education as taught. One way of helping to bridge the gap between character education being taught and character education being caught is to explore ways in which character development may also take place through the other areas of the curriculum, which is the aim of this chapter.

This chapter is based upon the National Curriculum of 2015 for primary schools in England. Immediately, there are two points to recognise about this choice of structure. Firstly, it is acknowledged that there is a range of other curricula for primary years, such as those in Montessori, Reggio Emilia and Steiner schools as well as the Primary Years Programme of the International Baccalaureate. Each of these has its own philosophical underpinnings which may be more or less consonant with character education. Secondly, national curricula decided at a central government level seem to be under more sway from the influence of Secretaries of State than curricula offered by non-governmental bodies such as the IB. This inevitably leads to their content being less stable over time as successive governments place their own emphases on different educational ideas. This is a familiar challenge to teachers in UK state schools and it also presents a challenge to them in bringing a stable philosophy and practice such as character education to bear on content which may change in five or ten years' time. If schools take the decision to bring character education to bear on the curriculum itself, teachers will need to find ways of making it fit within existing philosophies and structures, and also of doing it in such a way that it won't have to be re-written (too often!) in the future when statutory content appears in or disappears from the curriculum.

The primary National Curriculum makes it clear that the statutory content is where planning for educational content begins, and that there is room for surrounding it with other learning philosophies and opportunities:

> *The national curriculum is just one element in the education of every child. There is time and space in the school day and in each week, term and year to range beyond the national curriculum specifications. The national curriculum provides an outline of core knowledge around which teachers can develop exciting and stimulating lessons to promote the development of pupils' knowledge, understanding and skills as part of the wider school curriculum.*
>
> (Department for Education, 2014, p.5)

As will be made clear below, the National Curriculum itself is replete with references to what might be considered the development of virtue and character across the 13 statutory curriculum areas (including RE and PSHE). As was argued above, character development is an inevitable outcome of schooling: the challenge for educators is to make that character development deliberate and well-organised. There will be different reactions amongst primary teachers to the suggestion that there is room in the curriculum to cover other matters; however, the document itself allows room for the specified content to be swallowed up and completed by a philosophy of education which is coherent with it. The aim of this chapter is to show that character education is one such philosophy and practice.

The backbone of the chapter explores how character education can be approached through the teaching of English and the following sections look at the contributions that the other specified subject areas can make.

Teaching character through English

The teaching of English through language, literacy and literature has significant potential for helping children to understand virtue and character development. The demands of the acquisition of virtue, such as emotional understanding and the giving and taking of reasons, as well as performance virtues such as persistence, determination, resilience, paying attention, precision and being methodical, are inherent in the current primary National Curriculum for English, Language and Literacy as these extracts demonstrate:

- '[Pupils] should learn to justify ideas with reasons'.

- 'Pupils should develop the stamina and skills to write at length, with accurate spelling and punctuation'.

- 'A high-quality education in English will teach pupils to speak and write fluently so that they can communicate their ideas and emotions to others and through their reading and listening, others can communicate with them'.

- 'Through reading in particular, pupils have a chance to develop culturally, emotionally, intellectually, socially and spiritually. Literature, especially, plays a key role in such development.'

- 'Pupils should be able to adopt, create and sustain a range of roles, responding appropriately to others in role. They should have opportunities to improvise, devise and script drama for one another and a range of audiences, as well as to rehearse, refine, share and respond thoughtfully to drama and theatre performances.'

What is sadly missing from the curriculum is an explicit requirement for using English to help children to grow in *moral* understanding. Detailed work has been done on teaching the moral virtues through story, for example the Jubilee Centre's *Knightly Virtues* project and the writing of Karen Bohlin (2005) and Carr and Harrison (2015). One area where character education can extend the requirements of the national curriculum is in using the teaching of English to help children to know the good, value the good and do the good. There is also no statutory requirement for young people to use their learning in English to develop civic virtues. Composition is an excellent vehicle for children to learn how to persuade others to do something about local, national or international political issues.

The following sections explore how English can be used to develop children's emotional, moral, performance and civic virtues.

The emotional content of stories

One of the delights of reading or listening to a story is the capacity of narrative to provoke meaningful emotional experiences. These experiences can create deep and long-lasting memories within us, not only as a result of our imaginations transporting us to different realities, but also as our emotions respond to our imaginations by creating new landscapes of feeling.

Learning to feel the right thing, at the right time, in the right way, towards the right person, for the right reasons is central to character education and as teachers, stories provide us with a wonderful resource to help children learn this.

One of the start points in this learning is being able to identify what emotion(s) we are feeling at any given moment. A simple tool that can help us to do this is called a mood map, which is based on James Russell's '*circumplex model of affect*' (1980):

The vertical line describes the amount of adrenaline in the body, from low to high and this relates to how much energy we feel we have. The horizontal line describes how much serotonin is present in the body and relates to how 'good' or 'positive' we feel. The further you move from top to bottom or from left to right, the more intense the presence of adrenaline or serotonin respectively. The lines intersect to give us four zones, clockwise from top right: the 'performance zone': high energy, positive energy; the 'recovery zone': low energy, positive energy; the 'burnout zone': low energy, negative energy and the 'survival zone': high energy, negative energy. Some emotion words have been included on the diagram in Figure 6.1 to illustrate how it works.

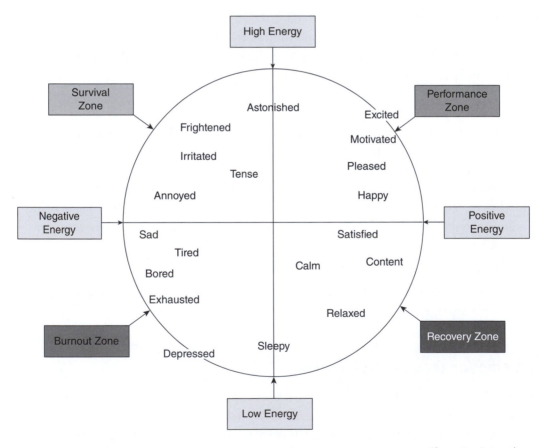

Figure 6.1 A mood map

The map enables us to plot our mood at any given moment, either by recognising how our bodies feel, or by identifying with an emotion word on the mood map.

This can be a very powerful tool in enabling children to recognise the emotional impact that stories have on them. As children sit and listen to a story, each child has a mini-whiteboard with a mood map so that they can plot points on the map as they become aware that they feel particular emotions. This can then open up discussion about what elements of the story elicited particular emotions in individuals and also help children to recognise that we can each respond with different emotions to the same stimulus.

It could also be useful for helping children to develop empathy. Asking them to track the emotions or moods of characters in a story using a mood map and then explaining their observations afterwards can help children to take the imaginative leap from how they are feeling to how another person is feeling.

Learning to become aware of and regulate our own emotion is of central importance in character education, as the moral virtues manage our feelings and desires to bring about good outcomes. Stories, language and literacy can not only be used to help children to learn about their emotions, but also reflect on what makes for a morally sound decision and what doesn't. It is this moral aspect of teaching English that we turn to next.

The moral content of stories

Stories invite us into a world of characters who have to make decisions with implications of right and wrong, good and bad, benevolence and harm. As children become absorbed in the lives of the characters they encounter in stories, we have an opportunity to develop skills of moral reasoning.

Chapter 5 used the example of *The Lorax* by Dr Seuss. This short story has two main characters: the Onceler and the Lorax. The Onceler is a businessman who discovers that he can use truffula trees to make thneeds, an item of clothing which soon everyone wants. The Onceler displays vices such as greed, rudeness, ignorance and selfishness as he exploits the natural world for his own profit. The Lorax is an animal who lives with other species amongst the Truffula Trees and is worried as the Onceler fells the truffula trees and pollutes the environment, affecting his friends' habitat. He displays virtues such as courage and persistence as he tries to persuade the Onceler to stop ruining the environment. In reading or listening to the story, children can build up their virtue knowledge (and meet literacy targets by acquiring new vocabulary) and start to see what certain virtues and vices look like. They can then apply this virtue knowledge acquired from fiction to their own lives.

On one reading, the moral message of the story is simple and the virtues and vices are clear. Children can work with closed questions about the text (e.g. 'what did the Onceler do?') and open questions (e.g. 'what was bad about what the Onceler did?'), and start to draw their own moral conclusions about the characters. They can also speculate and hypothesise about different possible endings, such as if the Lorax had been able to persuade the Onceler, perhaps using role-play to enact these different endings. This provides children with the opportunity to give and take reasons, justifying what they think with further explanation. This giving and taking of reasons about the story can then be applied to the giving and taking of reasons about real moral issues such as our desire for cheap clothing being met by people having to work for very low pay in appalling conditions, or how our desire for some consumer goods means that the environment suffers.

Because the story doesn't involve the direct breaking of obvious rules or laws, it can also be used to introduce the ideas of moral complexity and ambiguity. The Onceler seems to display virtues such as persistence and ingenuity. The Lorax, it could be argued, displays cowardice as he doesn't do everything he can to stop the Onceler and instead seems to resign himself to the environmental fate that befalls him, in the meantime doing nothing more than speaking sternly to the Onceler. This enables us to explore the question of whether actions are virtuous if they are directed at bad ends, or if they are virtuous if they don't achieve good outcomes (the idea of tragedy). The story can also open children to the reality that people are not wholly good or wholly bad, that heroes are not all powerful, that maybe one can be heroic just by doing the best one can, and that villains might be able to redeem themselves.

Just as responding to stories can create opportunities for character education, so too can creative writing or the keeping of a journal. The primary National Curriculum requirements for Year 3 (ages 7–8) include that children are able to create characters, settings and plot in their own narratives. One way of assisting children to do this is for them to invent characters using the building blocks of virtues and vices which they will have encountered by deconstructing the characters they come across in stories that they read or hear. By beginning with groups of virtue words and vice words, children can create characters from scratch, place them in an environment and then begin to provide their characters with experiences (plot) which bring out the virtues and vices they have given them. This enables them to build up their virtue knowledge, virtue reasoning and virtue practice, as well as experimenting with communicating emotion to an audience.

For generations of primary children, Monday morning has begun by sitting down and writing about what happened over the weekend. This activity can be used to develop virtue knowledge, virtue reasoning or virtue practice (see Chapter 5) in a way that doesn't interfere with the wonderful free-hand nature of the exercise, by giving children the task of including at least one virtue word in what they write. All of our experiences are shot through with elements of virtue and vice and journaling offers a good opportunity to observe virtue, name it, understand it and reflect upon it.

Performance virtues and English

Learning to read and write is hard and it takes sustained practice over a long period of time in order to master it. A child's success in learning to read and write in no small part depends upon performance virtues such as persistence and determination. Teachers have a great opportunity to help children to learn to identify these virtues and be able to call upon them when they are required. Performance virtues rely upon our becoming aware of our emotional states when something is too difficult (e.g. anxiety, frustration) or too easy (e.g. boredom) and learning what to think and do in those situations. For example, if a child becomes frustrated when she is reading something challenging, she first of all needs to become aware of how frustration manifests itself in her feelings and behaviour, perhaps by using the mood map illustrated above. The feeling of frustration tells us that we *perceive* a situation as difficult; this can then lead us to simply give in to frustration and give up on the challenge, or it can motivate us to try to think about the challenge in new ways so that we remain engaged with it; for example, 'I am finding this difficult, I can ask someone for help', or 'I am finding this difficult. The last time this happened, I tried X and it worked'.

We don't just work out performance virtues on our own: we learn them from others. One way that children can acquire performance virtues is to engage in dialogue with their peers as they face and overcome similar challenges, with the knock-on consequence of helping to create a community of learners and enquirers who support each other. The importance of this is recognised in the primary National Curriculum for English, as a statutory requirement for Year 6 is for children to evaluate and edit by assessing the effectiveness of their own and others' writing.

One example of this in action is the Expeditionary Learning Schools where Ron Berger has done so much of his work. In his book *An Ethic of Excellence* (2003), he describes creating a culture of craftsmanship in the classroom, by encouraging children to give very specific feedback – he calls it critique – on each other's work so that they can re-draft and improve it. Telling someone else what they have accomplished and what they need to do more of, and avoiding giving compliments masquerading as feedback, can enable children to learn that doing something well takes time and may involve mistakes and several attempts and it also helps to initiate them into performance virtues such as persistence, precision, flexibility, acting on feedback and paying attention to detail. Berger employs three rules with his pupils when they are giving feedback:

1. 'Be kind': the critique environment needs to be safe and not hurtful or sarcastic.

2. 'Be specific': 'no comments such as *It's good* or *I like it*; these just waste our time.'

3. 'Be helpful': the goal of the critique is to help the individual and the class, it is not about the critic having their voice heard, or 'cleverly pointing out details that are not significant to improving the work.'

Berger then goes on to explain some guidelines which he gives to his pupils to assist them in giving constructive critique, such as beginning with the pupil explaining his/her own work, the critique beginning with something positive about the work and then moving to constructive criticism, and the comments focusing on the work, not the person. The critiques take two formats: *gallery* and *in-depth*. Gallery critique involves the whole class sharing their work, and in-depth critique focuses on one specific piece with the aim of improving it. Notwithstanding the sophisticated level of moral and civic virtues required for whole classes to work together in this way, Berger's emphasis on constructive feedback and re-drafting a piece until we are proud of it creates an extraordinary opportunity for developing performance virtues such as flexibility and persistence, and learning that something of value is rarely perfect first time. A nice example of this process in action is given in Berger's short video *Austin's Butterfly*, which can be found online at https://www.youtube.com/watch?v=PZo2PIhnmNY.

All areas of the curriculum provide children, in conjunction with their peers and their teachers, with the opportunity to acquire and develop the performance virtues, because learning across all disciplines involves varying degrees of stretch and challenge and because children do not all find the same types of learning challenging. The principles of children becoming aware of frustration, anxiety or boredom when they experience those feelings, and then being able to do something to get themselves re-engaged underlie all learning.

English and civic virtues

One of the most common uses of language is in our attempts to persuade others to come round to our point of view. The ability to persuade is based upon developing sound arguments and selecting the right language forms for our audience, but above all it is based upon awareness of moral issues in our communities, a desire to do something to make a change and the belief that change will come through our efforts.

The teaching of English, particularly through written and spoken English, has a significant role to play in bringing these civic virtues to life by enabling children to identify issues they would like to do something about and equipping them with the written and spoken language tools to do so. This work can take a variety of forms from letter and email writing, to the creation of webpages and blogs; from presentations in front of a class, to pieces of drama performed to a much wider audience. Campaigning on social issues, however, should not be seen instrumentally as a way of meeting curriculum attainment targets (even though it does this), but should instead be seen as an apprenticeship in becoming socially engaged and socially active and preparing children for a good life beyond school.

Social action also draws upon learning from other areas of the curriculum. Persuasive arguments often depend upon the gathering of reliable data and statistics, which in turn depends upon numeracy. A number of issues people choose to campaign about, such as the building of wind farms for example, depend upon accurate scientific understanding, which in turn may have geographical implications. The study of history, especially the local study now specified for Key Stage 2, can be used to track the development of an issue within a community, understanding its impact over time and comparing with historical examples from elsewhere.

This chapter has so far focused on the contribution that can be made to character education through the teaching of English. The whole curriculum, however, has a contribution to make to this project and the remainder of the chapter explores some of the ways that other subject areas can be used to help to develop virtue and character, using the Primary National Curriculum as stimulus.

Teaching character through other subjects

Mathematics

As mentioned above, the development of the performance virtues can take place across the whole curriculum, but mathematics may have a particular role to play. Getting to grips with the conceptual understanding of manipulating number can be very challenging for children and it depends not only upon actually understanding the maths itself, but upon developing attitudes to learning which will enable them to pay close attention to detail, be precise, be flexible in their thinking, not give up when mistakes are made, ask for help, increase the challenge if they are bored and manage feelings of anxiety or frustration when the task becomes difficult.

The acquisition of these performance virtues takes skilful guidance from teachers who themselves don't become frustrated when children aren't learning, but instead try to help children master their feelings and thinking so that they can re-engage with the task at hand. Simple systems such as traffic light cards (where green means 'I'm learning', amber means 'I'm struggling, but working on a solution', and red means 'I'm stuck') can help overcome the challenge of meeting the needs of 30 children at once, by giving targeted support. The system also gives children the opportunity to tune in to their feelings and communicate them. Peer learning/mentoring can also help children recognise that their friends can help them to overcome their frustrations and get on with learning.

Maths can also help in gathering information for discussions of moral issues such as justice and fairness. Being able to identify whether a resource has been distributed in the right amounts to the right people relies upon maths and can develop in sophistication from simple numbers through to ratios, percentages and fractions.

Science

Steps one and two ('stop' and 'notice') of the caterpillar process explained in Chapter 5 overlap significantly with helping children to develop as scientists. The primary National Curriculum for science states as an aim: *'The principal focus of science teaching in key stage 1 is to enable pupils to experience and observe phenomena, looking more closely at the natural and humanly-constructed world around them. They should be encouraged to be curious and ask questions about what they notice.'* Growth in virtue across all four domains depends upon being able to pause and gather more information with an attitude of curiosity and to then offer up hypotheses for what our observations mean.

There are also some specific areas of the science curriculum which raise issues of virtue:

- The Year 4 curriculum requires children to understand that environments can change and that this can pose risks to living things. This study can lead to the moral and civic virtues associated with caring for the environment and drawing resources from it in a sustainable way.

- The Year 5–6 curriculum requires children to understand the changes in humans as they progress to old age. A character education focus could explore how particular habits (e.g. exercise or smoking) lead to different developments into old age, or could question whether virtues are observable to scientists.

- The Year 6 curriculum specifies a study of the effects of lifestyle upon health. This can also be studied as a moral or civic issue, where scientific facts about the impact of smoking or poor diet could be used to come to moral conclusions about whether substances like tobacco or sugar should be more heavily taxed or banned altogether. This can lead to a civic virtue study in what children can do to lobby particular groups for changes to legislation.

- The Year 6 curriculum also specifies a study of how offspring are similar to their parents, but not identical. This provides an opportunity to study not only physical similarities, but similarities in temperament and/or virtue and investigate whether parents have a measurable impact on the kinds of virtues their children display.

Art

In many ways the study and practice of art is similar to the study and practice of English, because so many works of art tell stories which have moral implications. Art also provides opportunities to develop the performance virtues because of the scope to engage in challenging projects over time and to modify our work in the light of constructive feedback. There are some specific areas of the art curriculum which provide opportunities for character education:

- The KS2 curriculum specifies that children begin to keep sketch books. In the same way that the keeping of a written journal can help children to make observations about changes in character over time, so too a sketch book can give them the opportunity to explore virtue and character pictorially.

- The art curriculum also introduces children to the work of recognised artists. As mentioned above, much of this work contains moral themes which are appropriate for primary aged children to explore. The lives of famous artists are also full of tales of virtue and vice:

for example Leonardo da Vinci's illegal dissection of human corpses to better understand how the human body worked.

Computing

As with maths, computing provides opportunities to acquire the performance virtues with its requirements to understand logarithms and create and de-bug simple computer programmes.

The requirements in Key Stages 1 and 2 to learn how to use technology safely and respectfully raise very important moral and civic questions of kindness, cruelty and trust. Becoming an effective user of search engines requires the intellectual virtue of being able to discern between useful and useless information as well as being able to identify reliable sources.

Design and technology

Designing an artefact that will be useful to others depends upon the virtue of empathy and a good understanding of how to meet someone else's needs, which comes about through careful listening to the target market. DT can help to develop performance virtues as children translate designs into artefacts and discover how to cope with mistakes that they have made. The DT curriculum also specifies that children learn how to prepare healthy meals, and come to an understanding of seasonality of produce. This opens the way for a study of moral virtues to do with the habits of healthy eating, and the sustainability and ethical provenance of the goods we use when preparing our meals.

Geography

Geographical understanding underpins almost all moral issues, because moral issues occur in human and physical geographical space. The migrant crisis currently troubling politicians in 2016 makes no sense in the absence of an awareness of the geographical implications. The KS2 Geography curriculum creates specific opportunities for linking moral issues to geographical awareness by requiring a study of physical geography, which could include a focus on natural disasters or global warming, and a study of human geography, including the distribution of resources such as food and energy, which should inevitably include a discussion of whether or not those resources are distributed fairly or sustainably.

History

Through investigating the events of the past, children can be invited to enter into an exploration of the vices and virtues of some of the key players in human history from a range of civilisations. Not only can they develop the intellectual virtues of precision, identifying reliable sources and trying to match stories to the known facts, but they can also explore the moral landscape of certain historical events and ask questions about how events may have been different in the presence of different characters. The local study in Key Stage 2 can be used to explicitly develop performance virtues such as collaboration, persistence and attention to detail.

Languages

The curriculum for language teaching in Key Stage 2 is full of references to the different performance virtues which support the acquisition and speaking of a foreign language, and especially of speaking it in public in the early days of learning it. Highlighting performance virtues such as listening attentively, joining in, responding to opinions of others, seeking clarification and help, accuracy of pronunciation and intonation, and reading carefully can help children learn what it feels like to deploy those virtues successfully and find ways of transferring them to other areas of their learning.

Music

In a similar way to languages, music can help children to develop performance virtues as they learn to build their skill with something unfamiliar and through learning to develop the 'confidence and control' to perform musically in public. The curriculum also specifies the learning of elements of music history, which can create opportunities for learning how music is connected to moral issues. For example a study of the origins of some forms of music can show how they were a response to oppression and poor living conditions (e.g. blues or hip hop).

Physical education (PE)

PE provides lots of opportunities for highlighting not only the technical virtues of building skills in a particular game or discipline, but also the performance virtues associated with gradually improving skill over time and learning from feedback and the moral and civic issues of playing fairly, observing rules and offering support rather than belittlement to players who are finding a game difficult. The curriculum also stipulates a requirement for outdoor and adventurous activity which can be an excellent opportunity for helping children to become aware of and manage their emotional states when facing risk or danger as well as learning to support peers through challenging situations.

Religious education (RE)

RE is in a slightly unusual position in the National Curriculum, as the content for the subject is decided locally in the Locally Agreed Syllabus. This means that there will be considerable variation from region to region in the content of the RE syllabus, and depending upon whether schools belong to a faith community. That said, RE provides golden opportunities for exploring the virtues as most RE curriculums involve a study of the lives of religious leaders, religious texts, religious practices of believers and a study of ethics. All of these different areas lend themselves to a study of the virtues in action and can be of particular help to children in reflecting on how they might like to emulate the virtues of religious leaders or religious believers, without necessarily adopting their faith position.

Chapter summary

This chapter has given a brief sketch of how the curriculum as a whole can be used in the primary school classroom to bring character education to life. To give children the best chance of understanding what virtue is, how utterly relevant it is to them at all stages of life and how they can develop autonomy and agency in becoming more virtuous, schools should give serious consideration not only to teaching character as a discrete subject, but also of finding ways of showing that it is present in and indeed indispensable to the curriculum as a whole.

Further reading

Arthur, J., Harrison, T. and Wright, D. (2014) *Teaching Character Through the Curriculum*. Birmingham: University of Birmingham. Available from: www.jubileecentre.ac.uk/userfiles/jubileecentre/pdf/Teaching_Character_Through_The_Curriculum1.pdf

This publication, although primarily aimed at secondary schools, demonstrates how character might be taught through 14 secondary school curriculum subjects. The links between character virtues and the pedagogical practices and content of each subject are also explored. For each subject, the virtues that might be considered most closely linked to it are emphasised and learning and teaching activities that develop character virtues in the classroom, across the whole school and in the community are suggested.

References

Berger, R. (2003) *An Ethic of Excellence.* Portsmouth, NH: Heinemann.

Bohlin, K. (2005) *Teaching Character Education Through Literature.* London and New York: RoutledgeFalmer.

Carr, D. and Harrison, T. (2015) *Educating Character Through Stories.* Exeter: Imprint Academic.

Department for Education (2013) *The National Curriculum in England Key Stages 1 and 2 Framework Document.* Available from: https://www.gov.uk/government/uploads/system/uploads/attachment_data/file/425601/PRIMARY_national_curriculum.pdf (accessed 15 January 2015).

Department for Education (2014) *The National Curriculum in England Key Stages 3 and 4 Framework Document.* Available from: https://www.gov.uk/government/uploads/system/uploads/attachment_data/file/381754/SECONDARY_national_curriculum.pdf (accessed 9 December 2015).

Russell, J.,= (1980) *A Circumplex Model of Affect.* Available from: www2.bc.edu/~russeljm/publications/Russell1980.pdf (accessed 6 November 2015).

7 Assessing and evaluating character education

In this chapter you will:

- learn how to assess and evaluate character education;
- have some points of caution flagged up about issues relating to successfully measuring pupil progress in character education;
- learn about what should be assessed;
- be provided with a strategy for assessing progress in virtue learning and development.

Introduction

The purpose of this chapter is to provide some ideas about how we might go about assessing character education. The two main strands to this idea of assessment are firstly how teachers can enlist pupils to assess and provide feedback on the effectiveness of character education materials and secondly how assessment descriptors may be used to help children to grow in understanding of how virtue is acquired.

As outlined in Chapter 3, there are some notorious problems with the measurement of 'character' and 'character education' and whilst some ingenious solutions to the measurement problem are being suggested – notably by the Jubilee Centre at the University of Birmingham – effective measurement of the impact of character education initiatives may be beyond the time and resources of many primary schools.

That said, there are some simple ways that schools can make use of existing approaches to assessment and reporting that can enable them to get a temperature check on pupil and staff perception of character education provision and pupil progress with the acquisition of virtue and character.

Is it working? How do you know?

In the early stages of implementing a character education programme, feedback from the pupils is really important in gauging the success of the materials you put together. Children will tell you straight away through their body language and engagement levels whether or not the learning activities you have designed are any good. They will also tell you if you ask them. If you are open with the pupils about trying out a new subject with some new approaches to learning from the start, they will generally rise to the challenge of giving thoughtful constructive feedback to you. This should in no way undermine the authority of the teacher: children can benefit a great deal from believing they are part of a collaborative effort to design good learning materials and if the process is carefully led, you can transform the teacher-pupil relationship into what Paolo Freire calls problem-posing education where the boundaries between teacher and pupil change to teacher-learner and learner-teacher, where anyone in the class can occupy either role.

This process of feedback gathering needs to be done thoughtfully and gently. Children quickly (and rightfully) develop survey fatigue and useful feedback can be gathered through an informal discussion at the end of the session focusing on two simple questions: what went well, and what could be improved for next time? You could also ask a small group of children, representative of the class, to give you feedback on character education at regular intervals, again using very focused and structured questions which provide you with the information you need to make the sessions work better.

Another approach to discovering the impact of these lessons is to ask the children to write their own reports in character education. There are obvious practical constraints to this, but they can be overcome and children can write very powerful reflections on how the lessons have affected them and their learning. As with survey fatigue, it is important to limit the regularity of this reporting: twice in an academic year is probably enough.

There are two cautionary points to make at this stage, about grading of progress in character and the interior life of children. This is not the place to enter into the wider debate about the place of grading in our schools, but suffice it to say, it is utterly inappropriate for children to be awarded a grade (numerical or otherwise) for their character development. There is well-rehearsed research which shows that when giving children feedback, if the feedback comprises a comment and a grade, the children look at the grade and ignore the comment. If children receive a termly report on character where they are awarded a numerical grade for character development, how is the child to interpret that (assuming they won't read any summative/formative feedback)? What does that number mean to the child trying to widen their understanding of their moral agency in the world? It is also profoundly unhelpful to reduce the complexity of character development to a number (assuming it is even possible). In learning to acquire the habits of a good, virtuous life, I need specific feedback on how I handle my emotions, the reasons I give and take for my actions and the way my emotions and reasons translate into action *so that I can learn*. Numerical grades do not give specific feedback, either summative or formative.

Number grades also open the door for that most pernicious of phenomena: social comparison. Whether we like it or not, children compare each other's grades to establish some kind of hierarchy or pecking order. It would be counterproductive to the project of character education for children to get no further than placing themselves in a 'character hierarchy' based on numerical grades which don't mean anything. In giving feedback on character development we are seeking to provide very specific guidance to children so that they can acquire and develop certain virtues: numbers will not achieve this. We should also be aspiring to create a community of learners who are aware of their own character development, but who can also contribute to the character development of their classmates. Character development aims at helping children to realise the common human good and it is therefore a social enterprise. If a child is aware that she is working on regulating her fear so that she can participate in group work, she can ask for help from her classmates. In helping her to overcome fear, the classmates are in turn developing virtues such as compassion and persistence. Number grades and social comparison make this very difficult to accomplish.

The second cautionary note mentioned above concerns the interior life of the child. In *The Dangerous Rise of Therapeutic Education* (2009), Kathryn Eccleston and Dennis Hayes raise grave concerns about an anti-educational movement which assumes the emotional vulnerability of all children and which sees the role of education as being principally about 'kid-fixing'. In *therapeutic education*, Eccleston and Hayes suggest that there is a tendency for adults to go digging around in the interior lives of children, looking for problems which they can fix. This raises a boundary issue for character education which we need to be wary of as teachers. In teaching maths, I am on reasonable territory when interrogating a child's approach to solving mathematical problems in order to help them solve those problems better. When it comes to character development, there is the potential for asking much more probing questions about the nature of the self which we should be very wary of asking. As teachers, we ought to be clear about the distinction between what is visible (i.e. behaviour) and what is interior (i.e. thoughts and feelings) and not assume that the latter is open to us for interrogation. If a child wishes to keep their interior life private, that is to be fully respected.

What should we assess?

In Chapter 5, we saw that the basic building blocks of a taught course in character education are virtue knowledge, virtue reasoning and virtue practice, which can in turn be used to create a process of virtue development called *the caterpillar process*. These building blocks can be used to create an assessment framework, the primary aim of which is to assist children in becoming aware of their character learning *not* to provide assessment evidence for its own sake. It is important to reiterate that an assessment framework should exist to help children create a mental landscape of learning within a discipline so that they can make progress, not so that they can be ticked off or scored. It is also important to stress that the acquisition of virtue is a life-long project and not everyone is ready to embark upon it. Some children experience levels of neglect in their early years which will make it difficult for them to embark upon moral learning until their emotional development and attachment styles are repaired. In school age children, particularly at primary age, we are unlikely to see a child going beyond doing what is right through gritted teeth and being swayed by pursuing pleasure rather than doing what is right or good. This is in no way to denigrate the moral ability of children, who often surprise and inspire us with their perspicacity and wisdom. However, virtues are stable states of character and few children (and surprisingly few adults) will be at the stage where managing emotions, being in command of our desires and acting for the good are habitual, rather than exceptional. Moral development takes a long time. It is also not necessarily linear: just as we can develop good habits over time, so we can also fall into bad habits and undermine virtue learning that has taken place.

Set out in Tables 7.1 and 7.2 are the stages which describe what we might look for as we make progress with learning virtue. It is based upon the caterpillar process described in Chapter 6 and sets out the first three of six 'stages' of learning virtue.

As development in virtue becomes more sophisticated, we might see people progressing to stages 4, 5 and 6.

These descriptors can be used in a variety of ways to help children come to an understanding of what it looks like to employ a virtue. They might be used in discrete character education lessons, where children observe how these descriptors come into play: this can be done especially powerfully by using the characters from stories to help children gain understanding of how others are on a journey of acquiring virtue. They can also be employed across the curriculum so that children can gain understanding of how the virtues can support them in the study of the different subject areas.

The main intention behind the assessment of virtue is for children to grow in self-understanding and to help them to build the habits of living a good life. By involving children in assessing and feeding back on character education lessons, they can grow in understanding of what contributes to good learning about character and virtue. By asking children to write their own reports on character, you can open up their reflective vocabulary and self-understanding. Sharing assessment descriptors across the stages of developing virtue can help children to formulate a mental landscape of how virtue is developed and it can provide them with the drive to aspire to grow in virtue over a lifetime.

	Stage 1	Stage 2	Stage 3
Stop: pausing before moral choices are made.	• I didn't pause to assess the situation. I was carried into action by my emotions or my desires. • I was only interested in avoiding pain or pursuing pleasure.	• I found it difficult to pause to assess the situation. • I was too easily influenced by avoiding pain or pursuing pleasure.	• I paused to assess the situation. • I could resist the desire to avoid pain, but could not resist the desire to pursue pleasure.
Notice: awareness of the (moral) implications of a situation.	• I didn't notice what was going on, or that something was amiss.	• I was aware of what was happening, or that something was amiss.	• I was aware of what was happening or that something was amiss. • I had an understanding of the moral elements of the situation.
Look: understanding how emotions can help us to choose well.	• I was unable to identify my emotions, or the emotions of others.	• I was aware of my emotions and the emotions of others. • I wasn't able to use awareness of these emotions to act in the right way.	• I was aware of my own emotions and those of others. • I could use awareness of these emotions to try to act in the right way.
Listen: using reason to make deliberate (moral) choices.	• I could not identify the right thing to do in this situation. • I didn't know the middle way: the non-extreme actions. • I couldn't avoid making the same mistakes I usually make in situations like this.	• I had an awareness of the right thing to do in this situation, but was unable to do it. • I had an awareness of the middle way. • I found it difficult to avoid making the same mistakes I usually make in situations like this.	• I knew the right thing to do in the situation. • I could identify the middle way. • I was aware of the mistakes I often make in situations like this and tried to avoid them.
Caterpillar: understanding of personal (moral) development.	• I am unaware of the impact of my actions on the person I might become. • I would rather avoid pain or pursue pleasure than try to live life more skilfully.	• I was aware of the impact of my actions on the person I would like to become. • My desire to avoid pain or pursue pleasure makes it very hard for to me to live skilfully.	• I was aware of the impact of my actions on the person I am trying to become. • I can resist pain to live skilfully, but I find it harder to avoid pleasures.

Table 7.1 Stages of learning virtue – stages 1–3

	Stage 4	Stage 5	Stage 6: full virtue
Stop	<ul><li>I paused to assess the situation.</li><li>I could avoid pain to do the right thing, but might have been swayed by pleasures; ending up doing the wrong thing, even though I knew what the right course of action was.</li></ul>	<ul><li>I paused to carefully and deliberately assess the situation for its moral implications.</li><li>I may have desired to avoid pain or pursue pleasure instead of the good, but I could fully overcome these desires.</li></ul>	Stage 6 is like stage 5, but for the fully virtuous, doing the right thing happens without any effort of will: they take delight in doing the right thing.
Notice	<ul><li>I was well aware of what was happening.</li><li>I had a good understanding of the moral elements of the situation.</li></ul>	<ul><li>I was fully aware of the situation.</li><li>I had a full understanding of the moral elements of the situation.</li></ul>	
Look	<ul><li>I understood my emotions and those of others.</li><li>I could use those emotions to act in the right way.</li></ul>	<ul><li>I fully understood my own emotional response and those of others.</li><li>These emotions helped me to make the right choice about how to act.</li></ul>	
Listen	<ul><li>I had a clear idea of the right thing to do in this situation.</li><li>I had a clear idea of the middle way.</li><li>I could avoid the mistakes I have made in situations like this in the past.</li></ul>	<ul><li>I knew the right thing to do in this situation.</li><li>I knew the middle way.</li><li>I did not make the same mistakes I have made before, because I have learned from them.</li></ul>	
Caterpillar	<ul><li>I am aware of the person I am trying to become and understood how my actions would affect that.</li><li>I still find it hard to resist pleasures that hinder me from living really skilfully.</li></ul>	<ul><li>I know what kind of person I am trying to become and I choose how to act carefully because of this.</li><li>It is still sometimes an effort of will to do the right thing.</li></ul>	

Table 7.2 Stages of learning virtue – stages 4–6

Further reading

Nucci, L. P., Narváez, D. and Krettenauer, T. (eds) (2014) *Handbook of Moral and Character Education* (2nd edn). New York and London: Routledge.

This Handbook strives to replace the ideological rhetoric that infects the field of character education with a comprehensive, research-oriented volume that includes the extensive changes that have occurred over the last fifteen years. Coverage includes the latest applications of developmental and cognitive psychology to moral and character education from preschool to college settings.

References

Ecclestone, K. and Hayes, D. (2009) *The Dangerous Rise of Therapeutic Education*. Abingdon: Routledge.

Freire, P. (2007) Banking v problem-solving models of education. In Curren R. (ed), *Philosophy of Education: An anthology*. Malden, MA: Blackwell Publishing. pp 68–75.

Part 3

Character education – caught

This Part examines how good character is *caught* in primary schools. It contains four chapters, each exploring a different theme. Chapter 8 looks at the hidden curriculum and how to develop a whole-school approach to building character in pupils. Chapter 9 considers what makes a primary school teacher a character educator – as well as advice for ITT providers on preparing teachers for the role. Chapter 10 focuses specifically on the character building potential of some well-known and less well-known extra-curricular activities. A discussion of strategies useful for character coaching and reflection is also included here. The final chapter deals with approaches to drawing on resources in the wider school community to support with character education – including parents, the voluntary sector and business.

8 Whole-school approaches to teaching character

In this chapter you will:

- find out about the 'hidden curriculum' and its importance for ensuring character education is central to a school's vision and life;
- identify some key strategies for making the hidden curriculum more visible;
- discover how to develop a character-enthused school vision and mission statement;
- identify the responsibilities of school leaders and character coordinators for developing character education;
- learn why and how to involve pupils in developing the character education provision of a school;
- gain some advice on how to evaluate 'what works' in whole-school approaches to character education.

Introduction

The previous section explored ways in which character education might be taught in the classroom as part of a discrete or cross-curricular theme. As has been explained earlier, a distinction might be made between these more explicit approaches to character education, and those that are perhaps less visible and tangible and could be classified as more implicit approaches. Of course, although this explicit/implicit distinction is useful, there is a great deal of crossover between the two – and, importantly, they mutually re-enforce each other. For example, pupils who have learnt about different virtues might be more likely to look out for them around school. Likewise, pupils will notice a mismatch between a lesson on compassion and a school culture that is rife with cyber-bullying. This chapter attempts to describe what a school might do to establish a culture and ethos of character education. Belonging to a school community is a deeply formative experience; it shapes students' characters. This chapter explores how a positive school community is established in an intentional, planned, organised and reflective way, rather than it being assumed, unconscious, reactive and random.

Creating a culture of character education – the importance of the hidden curriculum

Positive school staff/pupil relationships are at the heart of good character education. An indication of when a school has a critical mass of such relationships is when it feels like a community rather than a collection of individuals going about their business. Positive relationships flourish in a positive culture and environment – one that is full of positive values. A school's culture is established and reinforced by many individuals – teachers, senior management teams, students and teaching assistants among others. It is communicated by many activities – assemblies, parents' meetings, corridor displays, websites and letters home, amongst others. Some schools seek to actively create a distinct culture in their schools and are explicit when it comes to communicating this vision. For example, some schools choose to develop a culture based on core values, and they do so in order to influence the character of their students. The 'It's Who You Are' report found that *character, virtues and values are best formed through a responsive whole school approach*' (Arthur *et al.*, 2006, p.12); whilst Arthur (2003, p.135) believes that *'schools need to agree a philosophical approach which is articulated in their mission statement, the policy statements and in the objectives for every subject'*. He goes on to suggest that *'the mission statement should be an outline philosophy and rational [sic] which describes the kind of human beings the school seeks to develop'* (2003, p.136), and argues that *'practices of character education need to be distinctive, whole school initiatives that are integrated into the school culture'* (2003, p.137). In their book *Building Character in Schools*, Ryan and Bolin (1999) talk about the need for schools to become 'communities of virtue'. They argue that a school ethos based on core values, that is clear and well communicated, can provide purpose, motivation and direction for both teachers and students.

The hidden curriculum is a term that is often used to describe the features that influence the culture of a school. The hidden curriculum is seen as distinct from, say, the content of particular lessons in the national curriculum. Often these features are not officially defined or written down; however, they become apparent in the way teachers describe their schools. Features of school life that relate to the hidden curriculum are as diverse as pupil/staff relationships, school rules, approaches to communication, teaching styles, learning environments, school buildings and architecture, behaviour management, reward programmes, uniforms, staff meetings, school policies and many others. All of these features and many others shape the social and cultural norms of any particular school. In particular they shape the values, attitudes, beliefs and habits of the staff and pupils and, as such, have a strong influence on a school's approach to character education. Through these features expectations on pupils' character are communicated – whilst they also help to shape the beliefs and attitudes pupils will take away with them from their time at school. The amount of time pupils spend in school means that schools will have a considerable influence on what character habits the pupils develop.

Making the hidden character education curriculum more visible

A school that aspires to be *a school of character* needs to demonstrate that it is being intentional, proactive and comprehensive in how it goes about the business of cultivating character in its pupils. This means going beyond an assumption that character education will simply happen. It involves taking active steps to build a school community that prioritises character and ensuring that everyone in the school buys into it.

For a primary school setting out on the journey of character education this would involve putting everything they do under the microscope – to evaluate how everyday principles and practices positively or negatively influence character. The following sections discuss those areas which need particular consideration.

The school vision for character education

Schools that are virtue driven have high expectations of their pupils and teachers. They are committed and determined to develop the character of their pupils through the articulation and demonstration of, and commitment to, core virtues. Many schools articulate these core virtues in mission statements. The big question is how are these articulated and do they actively live in the school ... or do they simply sit on a page of the school website. The first step to developing a character-centred mission statement is for schools to describe the kinds of future citizens they want to help develop, and then outline the philosophy and vision that underlies their approach. This mission statement should have clear links to the broader educational vision for the school – and make clear links to whole-school priorities such as attainment, pupil progress in literacy and numeracy, progress in the wider curriculum, behaviour and careers. This vision should include the ethical expectations on students as well as the types of virtues being prioritised (see Chapter 2). Once a draft mission statement has been developed it should be agreed by an inclusive and representative group of stakeholders in the school – which might include governors, teaching and other staff, parents and community members. It is also important to consult pupils, perhaps via the school council, on the mission statement to get their feedback and 'buy-in' early on.

Example character education school framework: Floreat Brentford and Hounslow

Floreat Education is an Academies Trust with two established primary schools in London, both of which opened in September 2015. Floreat's vision is rooted in a belief that society – enacted through schools – has a responsibility to cultivate children's cultural knowledge and

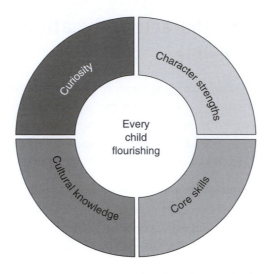

Figure 8.1 Floreat Schools' Every child flourishing model

their character development, alongside core skills in English and maths. In doing so, these two strands – often interlocking – provide an environment in which children can grow into the very best versions of themselves.

The trust has a Virtue and Knowledge School Model, which emphasises the development of pupils' character strengths as much as rigorous academic study.

Inspired by what the best primary schools do and extensively tested with educators, academics, parents and others, our curriculum will equip pupils with:

- Core skills: *developing literacy, numeracy and critical thinking skills enables pupils to access the entire curriculum.*

- Cultural knowledge: *discrete subject-based study allows pupils to deepen their understanding and engagement with the world.*

- Curiosity: *giving pupils the chance to apply their skills and knowledge in longer, more open-ended projects helps them to become more independent learners.*

- Character: *developing character strengths and virtues supports pupils' academic growth and helps them achieve personal wellbeing.*

We believe strong values are essential to flourishing. All Floreat schools will foster a core and balanced set of four virtues:

- *Curiosity – an intellectual virtue, that refers to open-mindedness, a desire to inquire, and a quest to improve and find out more.*

- *Honesty – a moral virtue, that calls on us to seek truth both in the world and within our own lives; this also calls for vulnerability and openness to feedback, whatever our status.*

- *Perseverance – a performance virtue that enables us to keep striving in the face of adversity in pursuit of long-term goals.*

- *Service – a civic virtue, meaning a commitment to help other people.*

Floveat Education Virtue and Knowledge
Core Values Statement

The role of school leaders

It cannot be overstated that schools of character have leaders (at every level) who have fully bought in to the importance of character education. A school's mission to undertake character education lives and dies by how committed the school's leadership is to it. However passionate a newly-qualified teacher is about character education it will never fully get off the ground unless this passion is supported and nurtured by those above and around them. Schools need leaders who understand the benefits of character education and want to take responsibility for establishing and promoting an ethos that emphasises it. This involves doing a number of things, including:

- being visible champions for character education;

- helping teachers understand that the greatest influence on the pupils' character is their own character;

- ensuring that all teachers are adequately trained to critically reflect upon and convey character education to their pupils;

- initially taking the leadership role in the development of a character-centred mission statement and ensuring that this is regularly reviewed;

- ensuring that character education is a central part of interviews and inductions for all new staff;

- taking active steps to ensure that the collective character of everyone involved reflects the school vision as stated in the mission statement;

- ensuring that every member of a school community (including all the professional staff) have some basic understanding of what character is and why it matters – this might be done through regular CPD sessions, twilight trainings and staffroom briefings;

- ensuring that character is taught through and within all curriculum subjects as well as other school activities;

- placing a strong emphasis on character education in school communications, including newsletters home to parents;

- making character a feature of assemblies and other whole-school activities.

The role of a character education coordinator

Although character education should be the responsibility of all teachers and staff in a primary school, some schools have created posts such as character education coordinators to bring organisation and leadership to the school's vision. In some schools this post is at a senior level – for example a deputy. The coordinator role might include:

- drawing up an annual programme of character-centered assemblies;

- organising staff training on character education;

- being in charge of evaluating character education provision;

- working with staff to ensure character education is taught through and within all other subjects;

- staying up to date with the latest research on character education and bringing findings about 'what works' into school practice;

- developing and delivering a discrete character education programme of study;

- developing strategies for closer partnership with parents and those in the local community on character education;

- organising real life opportunities for pupils to test their characters – such as volunteering activities, away days, challenges.

The role of all primary school staff

In order to inform and shape good members of society, or more precisely, children of good character, then all teachers and indeed staff in any school should have a role. To start the discussion about what this role should be, it may be appropriate during a staff meeting or INSET day that the school's current approach to character education is deconstructed and analysed. The school's curriculum plan or topic grids or long-term plan could be analysed, and underneath each subject section the subject co-ordinators could be asked to contribute ways their subjects could be linked to character education. This could be done as a way to empower staff, but more importantly to ensure a whole-school approach. This information could assist when writing a scheme and policy for character education.

Due to constraints of the National Curriculum at primary level and fitting all of the expected subjects into the timetable it proves difficult to allocate time to extra subjects. The senior staff, in consolidation with all, need to decide the best way to fit the teaching of character education into an already heavily-laden school schedule. This could be done through other subjects. For example, it may be worth continuing with existing approaches such as circle time to ensure that from Year 1 through to Year 6 the virtues identified are understood by all, that children know how these can be can be manifested, are articulated and interpreted.

As previously stated it may be worth developing a character education policy seeking out how character education is apparent already in subjects taught. By doing so you as a staff will clearly identify that character education did not take place prior to this. The doctrines and teachings of the faith, if you are working in a faith school, will obviously overlap, and all schools could include and start the policy with the school mission statement, as this underpins what you are all striving to achieve for the children – who should also be part of this process. In order to fulfil some of the suggestions for character education (see Character Education Primary Programme of Study, www.jubileecentre.ac.uk) and because of the ever-increasing demands of primary subjects, it would be useful initially to investigate where character education is already being taught. After all:

> *Though some of the key concepts, values and dispositions, and skills and aptitudes in the learning outcomes can be developed and applied within other parts of the curriculum, many of the skills and aptitudes, and knowledge and understanding need separate articulation. Nonetheless in primary schools this is likely to be done by class teachers through existing subjects and there can be substantial overlap.*
>
> (Crick, 1998, p. 52)

Involving pupils

As one of the main focuses of character education is to empower children, to enable them to reflect and consider correct choices later on in life, it is therefore important that they have a voice and an opportunity to participate in the planning of their school's character education provision. They must feel that adults and other pupils in the school will listen to their views. It is well documented that happy children perform and achieve well, or at least better than children who are unhappy. What could be happier than a child who feels they have a voice and can make a difference? Although the idea of children having a 'voice' is not new, considering a child's perspective as credible evidence on which to base decisions in education is a relatively recent concept. Wyness (2006) comments on the need to harness children's moral and social dispositions in order to achieve their successful future, so it seems only right that children's perspectives be considered when making decisions about character and values education. Indeed, the United Nations Convention on the Rights of the Child (United Nations, 1989) declares that everyone should be entitled to a fair hearing on matters which concern them, therefore in principle there should be no reason why children are not given the chance to participate in the decision about the character and values education they are provided with.

One way to achieve pupil voice on character education is through the School Council. Whatever term the School Council is in it may be worth, as a school, revisiting the constitution of such groups and considering how character education could apply to the running and organisation of the School Council. Many children may feel empowered when being permitted to visualise a democratic ethos throughout the school. The Crick Report (1998) discusses the use of school councils in order to promote a 'pupil voice' with the intention of involving children in the making of decisions that affect them, thereby giving them the autonomy and resulting in effective implementation (Crick, 1998). Whitty and Wisby (2007) also comment on the personalisation that a form of student voice allows children. However, when consulting children, the adults should be aware of the actual

Rung 8: Young people & adults share decision-making

Rung 7: Young people lead & initiate action

Rung 6: Adult-initiated, shared decisions with young people

Rung 5: Young people consulted and informed

Rung 4: Young people assigned and informed

Rung 3: Young people tokenized*

Rung 2: Young people are decoration*

Rung 1: Young people are manipulated*

Figure 8.2 Hart's ladder
*Note Hart explains the last three rungs are non-participation

level of involvement that they are allowing the child and the influence of the child's voice (Smith, 2010). The level of participation can be assessed using a model such as Hart's ladder (Hart, 1992); Nieuwenhuys (2004) notes that only the top rungs of the ladder actually involve the children in any decision making process (Smith, 2010). Again, when considering character education in schools it would be useful to fully involve the children in sharing the decision-making with regard to the character and values chosen to promote within the school; therefore when designing provision there is a need to consider rungs six and above on Hart's ladder.

However, it may be difficult for teachers to ascertain the process of defining character and values education or indeed to agree on a list of values to be debated. Therefore, with regard to the usefulness of the child's perspective in making decisions about character and values education, one must consider the evidence of when and if children have a sufficiently good understanding of morality, character and values to be competent when making decisions of this sort.

There is considerable empirical research to suggest that children's perceptions of values begin at an extremely young age, influenced in the first instance by their environment and the adults around them (Lin, 2010). Hay et al. (1991) observed sharing and Brownell et al. (2006) observed cooperation in young children, and each of these has been associated with the early development of values (Lin, 2010). Kohlberg (1970) describes a series of distinct stages in the moral development of children and young people, beginning with the pre-conventional level, where the determination of right and wrong is based on the consequences of actions without regard for moral judgements; through to judgements based on the considerations of individual ethics and logical reasoning at the post-conventional level. Whilst Kohlberg (1970) believes that the six stages should be gained in order, he does not determine the age or rate at which progress should be made. The *Learning for Life: Early Years* project (Arthur, Powell and Lin, 2010) gives examples of several instances where children's moral stage of understanding was put to the test and demonstrated that children between the ages of three and four were able to make choices based on a moral context that took into account the feelings of others as well as their own views.

Developing from this, the project *Character in Transition* noted that 10–12 year olds viewed the development of character and values as important to them, and they had a good moral awareness. Amongst those values held most important in this age category were trust and honesty (Arthur et al., 2010). These projects suggest that children of primary school age have a well-developed moral awareness and sense of the meaning of character and values. Given this evidence the ideas and opinions of pupils in the decision-making process should be listened to when it comes to choosing values that are important to them and relevant to their school.

Case Study: Developing a character-focused school mission statement alongside the pupils – Saint Michael's C of E Primary School, Middleton

Saint Michael's Primary school was one of the regional winners of the 2015 Department of Education Character Awards. The school endeavours to ensure that developing character goes hand in hand with high educational aspirations and achievement. They do this by striving to create a culture where staff are empowered to take risks and be inventive with the curriculum and learning, where mistakes are seen as a valuable part of the learning process, where all staff and governors support each other and the ethos of the school and, most importantly, where the relationships in the school between all stakeholders provide a secure foundation for skill development. Key to character development in the school is the pupils' mission statement that outlines its core values. The school recently worked with the pupils to rewrite the mission statement. This action was prompted after the headteacher asked the school council about the mission statement and, although they knew that it was on the walls in the classroom, they were unable to state any of its content. The headteacher developed a strategy to ensure that the pupils not only knew the mission and values but became the leaders of them. During assemblies and other sessions all the pupils compiled lists of what they thought was important about being a pupil at the school. The school council organised these into groups and composed a pictorial mission statement that represented the views and would be understood by all pupils, from 5 to 11 years old.

The schools core values in 'pupil friendly' language are:

- *Faith: Our Christian faith is at the very heart of St Michael's and runs through ALL aspects of school life.*

- *Striving to achieve our best: At Saint Michael's School everyone (pupils and adults) tries to be the best that they can be.*

- *Friendship: The children at Saint Michael's feel that it is important to be friendly to each other and also to any visitors that we have in school.*

- *Having Fun: It is very important that our school makes learning and playing fun, and that everyone likes to come to school.*

- *Helping Others: We realise that we are very fortunate and we try and find opportunities to help others.*

- *Learning: We are at school to learn and we will try our hardest to work with the teachers to make sure that we all achieve our potential.*

- *The 3 Rs: In everything that we do we will: Respect ourselves, Respect others, Take Responsibility for our actions.*

- *Tell the Truth: At Saint Michael's C of E primary School we always try to tell the truth.*

Evaluating character education provision and practice

To ensure that a primary school's character education provision is being effective it is important for teachers to undertake regular and honest evaluation of what is working. Just as important is to know what is not working. The evaluation should focus in on finding out if the character education vision, goal and aims of the school are being met. Before considering the approaches outlined below it is important to understand the challenges associated with measuring character as outlined in Chapter 4.

Different approaches might be adopted, or even better, combined to gain the clearest possible picture of what is working. These might include:

- interviews with teachers, pupils and parents to gain qualitative evidence;

- observation of in class and out of class activities providing a record of how learning is being infused with character education;

- inviting in teachers from other schools to provide an outside perspective;

- auditing lesson plans to see if they are infused with character education;

- using scales to try and get a before and after assessment of a particular intervention. There are some ready-made scales available to test virtues such as resilience, teamwork etc.; however, as most of these rely on self-report the results should be interpreted with caution;

- conducting a self-audit based on the ace principles (see www.character-education.org.uk);

- using surveys to collect quantitative data on things including pupils', teachers' and parents' perceptions of the culture and ethos of the school.

When combined, these different forms of evidence can be drawn together to provide a picture of character education in the school and can be used as a development tool for making changes and adjustments to current provision.

Chapter summary

Strategies to make the hidden curriculum more visible have been discussed in this chapter. The hidden curriculum is often where many of the everyday school practices that shape and inform the culture and ethos of a particular school reside. Strategies for ensuring a primary school is a school of character were outlined. These included: developing a mission statement on character education that staff can unite around; the importance of leadership buy-in; establishing a position of character coordinator; and how to evaluate and evidence success.

Further reading

Association of Character Education – 9 Principles for Schools of Character

ACE is the UK's subject association for character education. The organisation has established a set of nine principles for character education. These principles can be viewed on their website, www.teaching-character.org.uk.

References

Arthur, J. (2003) Education with Character: The moral economy of schooling. London: RoutledgeFalmer.

Arthur, J., Deakin-Crick, R., Samuel, E., Wilson, K. and McGettrick, B. (2006) *Character Education: The formation of virtues and dispositions in 16–19 year olds*. Canterbury: Canterbury Christ Church University.

Arthur, J., Powell, S. and Lin, H.-C. (2010) (3–6) *Foundations of Character – Developing character and values in the early years*. Available from www.learningforlife.org.uk (accessed October 2015)

Brownell, C. A., Ramani, G. B. and Zerwas, S. (2006) Becoming a social partner with peers: Co-operation and social understanding in one- and two-year olds. *Child Development*, 77: 803–21.

Crick, B. (1998) *Education for Citizenship and the teaching of democracy in school: Final report of the advisory group on citizenship*. London: Qualifications and Curriculum Authority.

Kohlberg, L. (1970) Stages of moral development as a basis for moral education. In Beck, C. and Sullivan, E. (eds) *Moral Education*. Toronto: University of Toronto Press.

Hart, R. (1992) *Children's Participation: From Tokenism to Citizenship*. Florence, Italy: UNICEF.

Hay, D. F., Caplan, M., Castle, J. and Stimson, C. A. (1991) Does sharing become interestingly 'rational' in the second year of life? *Developmental Psychology*, 27: 987–93.

Lin, H-S. (2010) It's hard to be a four-year old: Young children's moral encounters during their early character formation. In Arthur, J. (ed.) *Citizens of Character*. Exeter: Imprint Academic.

Nieuwenhuys, O. (2004) Participatory action research in the majority world. In Fraser, S., Lewis, V., Ding, S., Kellet, M. and Robinson, C. (eds.) *Doing Research with Children and Young People*. London: Sage.

Ryan, K. and Bohlin, K. (1999) *Building Character in Schools*. San Francisco, CA: Jossey-Bass.

St Michael's C of E Primary School, Middleton: Core values statement.

United Nations (1989) *Convention on the Rights of the Child.* Available from: http://www.ohchr.org/en/professionalinterest/pages/crc.aspx (accessed 20 December 2015).

Whitty, G. and Whisby, E. (2007) *Real Decision Making? School councils in action.* London: DCSF.

Wyness, M. G. (2006) *Childhood and Society: An Introduction to the Sociology of Childhood.* London: Palgrave Macmillan.

9 *Teachers as character educators*

> In this chapter you will:
>
> - learn how Initial Teacher Education (ITE) providers embed character education in their courses;
> - consider the role and responsibility of primary teachers in building character in their pupils;
> - learn about what it means to be a character 'role model'.

Introduction

Thomas Lickona (2005), one of the foremost experts in character education in America, notes *'the humanity of the teacher is the most important moral lesson in the character education curriculum'*. This chapter unpicks this argument and looks at the role and responsibility of primary school teachers as character educators. The chapter is based on the premise that teachers cannot simply be seen as technicians filling up their pupils' brains with knowledge detailed in a prescribed curriculum. They also need good judgement and professional autonomy in order to make decisions about how best to build each of their pupils' characters. This means accepting responsibility as a 'role model' and the need to set an example to their pupils about how to act and behave in different situations. This chapter considers what it means to be a 'character educator'. The chapter is principally concerned with how to support the initial professional preparation of teachers in primary schools in planning and delivering primary character education. This chapter is also relevant for all student teachers whether they follow a university route or a school-based initial teacher training route. The contents of this chapter will also be appropriate for practising teachers.

Routes into teaching and justification for character education

The teachers professional standards do not make any explicit mentions of character education. However, as will be discussed in the following section, character education is implicit through and within the whole teacher training process. The importance of character education in teacher education is also increasingly being emphasised. The Carter Review, initiated by the Secretary of State for Education, sought to identify which core elements of high quality ITT are key to equipping trainees with the required skills and knowledge to become outstanding teachers. The review made explicit references to character education and called for ITT to

provide new teachers with a grounding in child and adolescent development, including emotional and social development, which will underpin their understanding of other issues such as pedagogy, assessment, behaviour, mental health and SEND. ITT should also introduce new teachers to strategies for character education and supporting pupil wellbeing.

(Carter, 2015, p.23)

The Demos report entitled *Character Nation* (Birdwell et al., 2015) also made an explicit recommendation that government should ensure that initial teacher training covers the delivery of character education and moral reflection. A similar recommendation is also to be found in the APPG for social mobility report on character (Paterson et al., 2014). The Jubilee Centre has carried out a consultation on teacher education and character education which was developed in partnership with and endorsed by teacher educators across Britain. The key message to be drawn from the statement was that teacher education should acknowledge it has a responsibility to prepare teachers who prioritise both attainment and character development in their role. For many teachers this is common sense and most would argue that the hope and desire to 'transform' young people is the reason that they went into the profession.

The present Conservative government, and the previous Coalition government, have ensured that there are various routes into primary education which are increasingly school led and school managed. Currently there are four main routes into teaching:

- a traditional university-based route as a one-year Post Graduate Certificate in Education (PGCE) course or three- or four-year Bachelor of Arts (BA) course;

- the School Direct (SD) route, which is mainly school-led with some days at a university: these can be salaried or non-salaried;

- School Centred Initial Teacher Training (SCITT) with little or no time at university and mainly school-based;

- TeachFirst (TF) route, which is a two-year graduate scheme in challenging schools.

Following European legislation, all routes award Qualified Teacher Status (QTS) and some of the routes list above offer Master's credits, ensuring that the primary teaching profession retains its high professional status and is research-focused. Against this backdrop, the value of character education is both desirable and imperative in achieving a positive and inclusive atmosphere in primary schools, as evidenced by the Professional Standards (2012). The QTS (Training and Development Agency for Schools, 2007) are divided into three sections and in Part One we note the inclusion of:

- professional attributes;

- professional knowledge and understanding;

- professional skills.

The execution of a succinct set of standards, which are relevant to newly qualified teachers (NQTs) and recently qualified teachers (RQTs), as well as established and experienced teachers, will from the perspective of the government ensure:

> *an overarching set of standards establishes a platform for the coherent approach to Initial Teacher Education (ITE), induction and continuing professional development (CPD) that the profession aspires to.*
>
> (Training and Development Agency for Schools, 2007)

A recurring theme throughout the standards is respect towards all learners, enabling achievement and attainment on a broader scale. Part Two: Personal and Professional Conduct states it is important that:

> *{t}eachers uphold public trust in the profession and maintain high standards of ethics and behaviour, within and outside school*
>
> (Department for Education, 2011, p.10)

Indeed many of the standards explicitly emphasise positive values and behavioural expectations which are clearly linked to character education. Clearly this intangible aspect of 'trust' which is often 'caught' by children and young people is not formally 'taught'. Alexander (2010) and Ball (2006) argue that the ambiguity of standards and the reluctance to have transparent and clear modes of accountability are deliberately *'volatile, slippery and opaque'* (Shore and Wright, 1999, p.569) and open to interpretation. This policy contradiction will impact on the construction of teacher identity in relation to the professional judgement and autonomy needed to implement character education. Indeed:

> *the TDA framework is mostly unhelpful in the matter of discovering wherein the differences truly lie. This is because they focus on the teacher's possession of approved but vaguely-expressed information and skill, rather than on how the teachers might think; and whether the teacher conforms rather than demonstrates originality*
>
> (Alexander, 2010, p.415)

How teachers construct their identity and respond to the demands of performativity are embedded very early on in their careers. This is evident when they are student teachers in training, through the implementation of QTS (Ball, 2006), and by the strong and continued links to teaching standards which begins at the onset of their induction.

Also pertinent to character education are the National Priorities identified by Ofsted (see https://www.gov.uk/government/uploads/system/uploads/attachment_data/file/459282/ Initial_Teacher_Eduction_handbook_from_September_2015.pdf 2015). The priority areas for student teachers and all ITE providers are:

- managing behaviour and discipline;

- English as an additional language (EAL);

- special educational needs and/or disabilities (SEND);

- supporting underperforming groups of pupils;

- challenging bullying;

- making accurate and productive use of assessment;

- safeguarding and tackling extremism.

All of the above are closely interwoven with character education whether it is concerned with the primary teacher's moral responsibility to have a robust and accurate approach to assessment; an inclusive and fair approach to teaching all children; a fair and consistent approach to behaviour management; or upholding British values and displaying a commitment to social justice. Again some of these aspects will be 'taught' and some will be 'caught' via the conduct and manner in which the teacher presents him/herself. The various routes into primary teaching will have an impact on the future profession, especially considering how to prepare future professionals with the teaching of character education.

The complexity of reform in relation to Initial Teacher Education (ITE) is relevant when considering how to prepare future teachers to plan and deliver character education. Many academics have noted the increased pace of educational reform in the UK over recent years when considering the induction of new teachers to the teaching profession (Ball, 2003; Hardy, 2008; Levin, 1998; Tucker, 1999). For example, from 2010 onwards the Coalition Government introduced a wide range of policy initiatives to English primary education and the ITE sector, which claimed to simplify and enhance practice. The Academy Act 2011 was the fastest implementation of a Bill through Parliament in recorded history. However, it is argued that pedagogical and professional judgement, expertise and knowledge all related to character education have been eroded in English primary schools and replaced by an accountability culture established through administrative control (Elliot, 2004). This will have significant implications when one considers how teachers new to the profession will be involved in the development and implementation of character education. Trust in both teacher and ITE reform has been constructed in order that primary teaching and its outcomes can be managed and controlled, resulting in what Ball refers to as 'discourse of derision' (2001, p.17). What it is like to be a new teacher? And trusted as a professional who is responsible for teaching character education? Inevitably, it is complex, and within current rapidly changing education policy there is little evidence of trust in the teacher to develop and have autonomy on new initiatives such as character education (Arthur, 2013; Doherty and McMahon, 2007).

As a consequence, in the teaching profession it is now imperative to demonstrate high quality teaching as determined and judged by external agencies, collating evidence of QTS, as well as ensuring constant improvement of learning outcomes and attainment of pupils, leaving little room for teachers' perspectives. This has led to what Sachs refers to as a workforce of 'designer teachers' (Sachs, 2005, p.10) who are compliant to policy imperatives as well as having a blind acceptance of standard regimes. When primary teaching is reduced to evidencing academic knowledge or technical skills it neglects the fact that children and indeed all of us remember teachers for the kind of person they are rather than subject knowledge that they may have imparted to us. As Carr (2016) argues, a significant problem has been the recent promotion of technicist models of professional practice, which have sought to reduce teaching to the mastery of a repertoire of behaviourally conceived teaching skills or 'competences'. It is not possible to detail the full range of human abilities and qualities of a teacher within the concept of competence.

The implementation of earlier policies such as the codification of standards, performance management procedures and curriculum constraints (see School Standards and Framework Act, 1998) has already seriously impacted on teachers' daily practices and capacity to embrace new initiatives such as character education. Ball notes, '*the novelty of this epidemic reform is that it does not simply change what we, as educators, scholars and researchers do, it changes who we are*' (Ball, 2003, p.143). It is noted that such policies have a genuine effect on teacher morale and daily practices (Cooper and Olson, 1996; Beijaard et al., 2003; Tucker, 1999). Indeed in a recent survey by the Association of Teachers and Lecturers (ATL, 2015, p.1) it was discovered that almost three quarters (73 per cent) of students and NQTs have considered leaving the profession. Subsequently almost four out of ten teachers quit within a year of qualifying, with 11,000 leaving the profession before they have really begun their career (ATL). Therefore it is imperative for teachers new to the profession as well as established and experienced teachers to have support, guidance, and a framework for character education.

Case study: Character education in ITE at the University of Birmingham

Students studying for the primary Postgraduate Diploma in Education (PGDipEd) at the University of Birmingham (UoB) have a route that is mainly led by the university in partnership with selected schools in the region.

Teaching groups are small and students are encouraged to discuss and co-construct concepts relating to character education. Such topics are mainly located in professional studies sessions but as the team is small links are made in other areas of the curriculum in order for students to consider how character education can be taught through other subjects. For example, the English tutor is currently working on a scheme of work using Kohlberg's moral dilemmas (1976), and in mathematics the issue of ethics is outlined in terms of social justice when practical examples are shared with students, to inform their pedagogy of character education.

The course is very compact and to be compliant with the statutory guidance from the Department for Education (DfE, 2015), in being able to award QTS, UoB must ensure that students attend 120 days in schools. All primary schools who work in partnership with UoB attend and contribute to mentor training sessions at UoB in which the notion of *'taught'* and *'caught'* virtues, values and character education are analysed and critiqued. Many of the partnership schools have also significantly contributed to research for the UoB Jubilee Centre and student teachers have also been actively involved in research-based activities, thus highlighting the fact that the teaching of character education (and indeed all teaching) should be a research-based activity. Pedagogical approaches to teaching character have been investigated and student teachers, experienced teachers and mentors in partnership schools have worked alongside each other on projects at UoB's Jubilee Centre. These have included: *The Knightly Virtues Project, Attitude to Gratitude, The Good Teacher: Understanding Virtues in Practice, The Primary Programme of Study for Character Education, Thank You Letter Awards* and many more (For more information on these, visit www.jubileecentre.ac.uk/1610/character-education). Students' participant in such research not only has a positive impact on their knowledge and understanding of character education, thus contributing to their pedagogy, but it also adds to and influences their own academic work for the 120 Master credits awarded with the Primary PGDipEd. Recent events Primary PGDipEd students have taken part in have included the Character Matters Event, which was related to character in public and professional life, and involved David Blunkett, John Sargent, Lord Robert Winston and Dame Kelly Holmes. Being based at UoB offers students the opportunity to have sessions led by world-class experts such as Professor of Character Education Marvin Berkowitz (who is based at the University of Missouri).

In tandem with offering access to world-class researchers and a substantial amount of practice in schools, this unique course offers students the opportunity and space to consider aspects of character education which may be *'caught'*, through its small teaching groups and the Personal Tutor allocation. From the onset of the course students are asked to reflect on the qualities they have and need to develop so that they may become effective character educators. After these have been identified, the qualities are than discussed in tutorials with Personal Tutors during termly tutorials. Students are encouraged to take a reflective approach to their pedagogy, evaluate lessons taught, and collate evidence of QTS as well as deliberating on how to go beyond QTS. Going beyond QTS assists students to develop their own educational philosophy and has clear links to character education.

The utilisation of other agencies in order to lead sessions related to character education is also useful – these include West Midlands Police, Stonewall, and The Centre for Research in Race and Education (based at UoB).

Case study – Teaching phronesis in teacher education

Three new online courses, under the umbrella title 'Character in the Professions' are currently being developed and trialled by the Jubilee Centre. The courses' aim is to provide an online learning platform that teachers, doctors and lawyers can use to learn about character education and being a virtuous professional. The courses have been developed by the University of Birmingham and are free to use. They have been developed and trialled in partnership with teacher educators from across Britain. The courses have been developed as a response to previous research, conducted by the Jubilee Centre, which found that many training programmes for teachers, doctors and lawyers spent little or no time on why character matters and what it means to be a virtuous professional.

The course for trainee teachers aims to encourage them to think about their role as character educators. It explores a variety of complex issues including; how can teachers maintain their hopes and aspirations for becoming a teacher in the face of what they might see as competing agendas?; does technique-based training properly equip teachers for the complexities of the role and, in particular, when they face dilemmas?; how can a greater emphasis be placed on the moral importance of mentoring given restricted time when training?; how do we ensure that the team in which the professional works would expressly support virtuous behaviour and offer support and guidance to colleagues who lapse?; and, when things go wrong, how can we encourage the subsequent exploration to be about ethics and values rather than the mechanical aspects of 'who did what'?.

The course prioritises the theory of virtue ethics (see Chapter 4). This theory promotes the importance of personal character and virtues for making the right decisions, at the right time, in the right amount, in the right place with the right people. It focuses, in particular, on one central concept of virtue ethics – phronesis. Phronesis, often translated as practical wisdom, is the virtue professionals should seek to develop to help them become ethical practitioners.

The course is divided into three units and each unit consists of a series of steps. Within each step, an overview and some learning activities as well as some suggested additional learning resources are given. In unit 1 students learn what character and character education are, and they learn what virtue ethics and phronesis are. In unit 2 students get the chance to think about how they might apply phronesis to ethical dilemmas relating to their practice. Students consider the link between character, virtue and some of the public scandals in their profession. In this unit students also reflect on their own personal character strengths and how they relate to how they practise. Unit 3 is designed to encourage students to reflect on what they have learnt from the course.

For more information about the Character in the Professions courses see: www.jubileecentre.ac.uk/userfiles/jubileecentre/pdf/projects/Summaries/Interventions_with_Trainee_and_Student_Teachers_Lawyers_and_Doctors_Project-Summary.pdf

Teachers as character educators

The notion of character education being 'caught' is also similar to the 'hidden curriculum', a phrase used to consider the informal aspects of learning – not the formal curriculum but informal procedures which may convey certain unintentional messages. For example, if a teacher dismisses the girls before the boys each day before playtime – the unintentional message to the boys could be that the teacher prefers and is favouring the girls in the class. Another useful example is the timetabling of subjects – English and maths, in primary schools, are mainly taught in the morning, thus some children may not understand that indeed these subjects are relevant to all areas of the curriculum and are not just 'taught' or indeed 'learnt' in the morning. The conduct and character of each teacher may also be caught and be part of the hidden curriculum. As Carr points out:

> *It is often said that we remember teachers as much for the kinds of people they were than for anything they may have taught us, and some kinds of professional expertise may best be understood as qualities of character.*
>
> (Carr, 2007)

Primary school teachers are often viewed as social actors where their daily practices are concerned with performing in social and cultural contexts (Coffey, 2001; Rhodes and Greenway, 2010). Primary teachers' day-to-day practices are further complicated by the very nature of their role. For example, one significant factor is primary school teachers' contribution to children's construction of self-identities and character education, as influenced by the care and support shown by teachers and other significant adults around them. This links to the idea of teachers being '*in loco parentis*' and infers a need for teachers to care for children as successfully as parents would. Indeed, '*parenting remains the template for teaching at an unconscious level, and the process of teaching still works through a series of unconscious identifications*' (Shaw, 2004, p.56).

Primary schools are the places where children start to become pupils and where they learn how to perform as learners and how to contribute to society. As well as performing as learners, the socialisation into being an accepted member of a community also occurs in these settings. Primary school education plays a major part in shaping children's sense of self which is attributed to their character and which is often modelled by their class teacher (Millard, 2010). Bourdieu (2000, p.165) argues that when '*one becomes a miner, a farmer, a priest, a musician, a teacher or an employer {the process} is long continuous and imperceptible ... {and} starts in childhood*'. Against this backdrop, primary school teachers often find that their own identities and characteristics are intensely scrutinised, '*by pupils, parents, other teachers, governors and head teachers*' (Thornton and Bricheno, 2000, p.204), and as well as their professional practice being critiqued (Foster and Newman, 2005) their character is '*constantly being attended to by others*'

(Skelton, 2007, p.684). Thus, teachers need to be aware of the way in which they present themselves to the whole school community as well as children they teach.

The process of actively teaching character and values to children is a fairly new concept, having developed over the last 50 years from the work of Anscombe (1958), Wilson, Williams and Sugarman (1976) and Raths, Harmin and Simon (1966) amongst others. Hoyle (1969) notes that children begin to learn the acceptable behaviour and desirable values of their society from birth; doing so from those in their immediate social group, including their parents and siblings (see also Bronfenbrenner, 1979). This early socialisation enables young children to learn the desirable way to behave in order to do well within their society, as well as the development of children's character. No one is specifically teaching the child or necessarily referring to any of the vocabulary surrounding character and values education already discussed in this chapter. Nevertheless, in societies where there is no formal education system, it is claimed that the child still develops values, and such cultures have continued successfully without formal education of values for many thousands of years (Hoyle, 1969). Indeed, the formal education system in Britain is less than two hundred years old, resulting from the Education Act (1870). Before this, formal education was only available to the upper classes of society, yet there were enough people with decent values and good character to allow society to continue.

However, even as long ago as 1870, there was an awareness that in the ever changing, increasingly pluralistic society in Britain, complete character and values education could no longer be completely achieved by the family alone (Hoyle, 1969). This resonates with many of the debates around values driven and character education in contemporary discourse. In recent years, the dynamics of family life have been reshaped dramatically: society is ever more diverse and close communities with strict values based on culture or religion are increasingly rare (Arthur, 2010; Haydon, 1995). Pike (2011) and Kunzman (2015) describe how a person's own concept of values is likely to be influenced by cultural and community sources, including – but not exclusive to – religion. At the same time, Arthur (2010, 2015) comments on the decline of such organisations, meaning it is likely that, for some children, schools and teachers are the only sources of inspiration and direction when it comes to acquiring desirable values and forming a good character: schools have a central role to play in developing good character (Arthur et al., 2015).

Teachers as role models

If we continue with the theory that early in life, character and values are learnt from those around us, then the character and values educator must first be a role model for the child (Jubilee Centre, 2014). However, the child's view of teachers as role models remains controversial within the literature. Research by Thornton and Bricheno claimed that *'there is no indication that boys and girls identify with their teachers, male or female. They do not see their teachers as role models'* (2006, p.12). Research by Sanderse (2012) confirmed this and showed that role-modelling is rarely used as an explicit teaching method and that only a very small percentage of adolescents recognise teachers as role models. Sanderse argues that if role-modelling is to contribute to children's moral education, teachers are recommended to explain why the modelled traits are morally significant and how students can acquire these qualities for themselves.

Yet the literature portraying dominant representations of teachers needing to set an example to society and be role models has a long and enduring history. This is reflected in the work of Hoyle (1969), particularly in relation to expectations of primary school teachers. Hoyle's book, aimed at teachers and student teachers in England, refers to social norms and moral conduct as well as gendered expectations. The junior teacher is referred to as a *middle class, male who will behave in line with the norms which he will embody and seek to transmit to his pupils'* (Hoyle, 1969, p.25). The role of 'instructor' ascribed to a male teacher is in clear contrast to the function of his female counterpart for whom Hoyle states that *'one of her main tasks is to wean the child away from its psychological dependence upon the home'* (Hoyle, 1969, p.49). Although over 40 years old, Hoyle's recommendations and observations still chime with current policy initiatives in relation to the notion of what should be modelled by primary school teachers (see also Dermott, 2012, as well as McGrath and Sinclair, 2013).

Indeed the importance of primary school teachers *'as role models'* (Department for Education, 2013), is prevalent in policy agendas and is evidenced in the current QTS. Some suggest that to imply that a child would automatically identify with a teacher is *'ridiculously simplistic'* (Francis et al., 2006). Considerations of children as a homogenous group neglects the effects race, social class, and disability, as well as many other factors may have on identity. Nevertheless and notwithstanding this, primary school teachers will be influential people in the identity construction and character education of children they teach and care for. Notably lacking in the debate of teachers as role models are perspectives from teachers themselves, and it appears that *'as an academic community we appear to have little insight into how teachers experience primary teaching'* (Lyons, 2010, p.13). Therefore it may be worth asking staff at an INSET or a staff meeting to consider the virtues and values they feel they model to children and the school community in order to capture character education that maybe 'caught' by children in the school. Draper and O'Brien (2006) further argue that teachers' needs as employees are relatively invisible and their views, perceptions and understandings are often neglected in the planning and implementation of education policy. Recent research from the Jubilee Centre (Arthur et al., 2015) sought to redress this and asked a range of teachers at different stages in their career (student teachers, NQTs, RQTs and established teachers) for their perspectives on the personal qualities required to be an effective teacher. These included:

- fairness
- creativity
- humour
- perseverance

- leadership
- honesty

Similarly, in order to gain the perspectives of academics involved in the teaching and preparing of teachers of the future, the Universities Committee for the Education of Teachers (UCET) recognised some intrinsic characteristics which they believed vital for teachers to obtain and develop. The agreed 11 principles understood to be obtained and manifested in order to be an effective primary teacher are summarised below.

1. Intellectual integrity.
2. Vocational integrity.
3. Moral courage.
4. Altruism.
5. Impartiality.
6. Insight.
7. Responsibility for their influence.
8. Humility.
9. Collegiality.
10. Capacities for partnership.
11. Vigilance concerning professional responsibilities and aspirations.

(Tomlinson and Little, 2000, pp.152–4)

Likewise, Carr (2007) identified the qualities and dispositions that teachers may possess in order to encompass a professionally commendable approach to ensure overall effective teaching, as clearly very secure subject knowledge is important but not the only requirement for this to occur. He believes that teachers need to demonstrate that they are:

- trustworthy;
- respectful of others;
- fair;
- patient;
- loyal;
- principled;
- discreet;

- responsible;

- conscientious;

- good humoured;

- witty;

- optimistic;

- self-restrained;

- persistent;

- lively.

All of the above dispositions play a crucial role in primary teaching and it is important to note that the list is not an exhaustive list. Teachers are required to constantly reflect on their pedagogy and the progress of their children and whilst student teachers may be asked to evaluate their attributes and presentation of self, this becomes less prevalent as teachers qualify and begin their careers. Research by Sumsion (2000) notes that identity formation and character are not only influenced by what circumscribes an individual, but more crucially what colleagues and others anticipate from an individual and what they allow to affect their identity. This is particularly pertinent in the role model discourse which is often a method used to develop children's character education (Beijaard et al, 2003; Reynolds, 1997). This is important when one considers the character of each teacher in light of the lists above.

The ambiguous nature of character education means that up until now it has often been difficult to locate and the teachers are often referred to as role models in an attempt that some of the attributes above may be 'caught' by children. This can be problematic if it is unclear to teachers exactly what it is that should be modelled. Carrington and Skelton state that a role model is an outdated concept that '*has its roots in role theory, which was at its most prominent in the mid-1950s*' (Carrington and Skelton, 2003, p.255) and that '*there is no mention that teachers might, or should be seen as 'role models' to young people*' (Carrington and Skelton, 2003, p.255). As teachers are often referred to as role models there is a possible lack of a shared and firm understanding of the function of a role model amongst the community of primary school teachers, and indeed this is evident in education policy. According to Jones the notion of a role model is '*uncritically embedded,*' (2007, p.185) in the discourse of a primary school teacher's identity.

Alternatively, further interpretations of the notion of the role model are offered by Vescio et al., who suggest that it is someone '*to imitate, to be like*' (Vescio et al., 2004, p.2), which is further illustrated by relating role models to mentors and heroes. Marquese (1995, pp.9–10) outlines that role models are required to demonstrate that they have '*achieved personal success on the basis of the existing laws and customs of the society*'. When one considers the function of a role model through the lens of character education, the main tasks of a role model and what exactly needs to be modelled become clearer. Moreover once a shared understanding of character education and the values and virtues of each school have been established the easier it is for teachers to develop in their task of being a role model (please refer to the virtue definitions and virtue types earlier on in this chapter). Borba (2002) and Berkowitz (1997) agree that a child's view of role models develops with age and often extends to their teachers and peers when they begin school, while Clarken (2009) states that to be successful character educators, teachers must model the values that they wish to teach.

Whether or not teachers are considered role models by the children they teach, recent research by Arthur et al. (2015) found that 84 per cent of parents believed that the development of children's values should be encouraged by teachers in school, and 91 per cent of adults in a UK sample believed that schools have a role to play in the development of good character (Arthur, 2015, p.8). It is obvious that modern British society views schools as invaluable additions to the role of educating children in character and values (Arthur, 2015). The influence that a primary school teacher has on the children cannot be underestimated and the virtues and values modelled and demonstrated by primary school teachers will clearly impact on the children that teachers teach and care for.

Chapter summary

In this chapter there has been an attempt to form a greater understanding of the questions, debates and dilemmas posed relating to the initial and ongoing training of teachers with regard to character education. The chapter describes the responsibility of ITE providers to ensure it is embedded in their course and has provided some case studies as to how this might be done. The role of primary school teachers and how such teachers may position themselves in line with character education is also reported. Already established is the notion of what is *'caught'* and *'taught'* in relation to character education and this has been further developed in this chapter.

Further reading

Statement on Teacher Education and Character Education

(Available from http://www.jubileecentre.ac.uk/userfiles/jubileecentre/pdf/character-education/ Statement_on_Teacher_Education_and_Character_Education.pdf)

The statement on teacher education and character education was developed after a consultation with teacher trainers and trainee students as well as other interested parties across Britain. It makes the case for character education to be part of ITT as well as CPD. The statement provides a short and handy overview of the debate as well as summarising the key research.

References

Alexander, R. (2010) *Children, their World, their Education: Final report and recommendations of the Cambridge Primary Review*. Abingdon: Routledge.

Anscombe, E. (1958) Modern moral philosophy. *Philosophy*, 33 (124): 1–19.

Apple, M. W. (2006) *Education the 'Right' Way: Markets, standards, God and inequality* (2nd edn). New York: Routledge.

Arthur, J. (2010) *Of Good Character: Exploration of virtues and values in 3–25 year olds*. Exeter: Imprint Academic.

Arthur, J. (2013) Speech at Educational Doctoral Research Conference, 12th Annual Conference. University of Birmingham, 15 November.

Arthur, J., Harrison, T. and Wright, D. (eds) (2015) *Teaching Character through the Curriculum.* Available from: http://jubileecentre.ac.uk/userfiles/jubileecentre/pdf/Teaching_Character_Through_the_Curriculum1.pdf (accessed September 2015).

Arthur, J., Kristjánsson, K., Walker, D., Sanderse, W. and Jones, C. (2015) *Character Education in UK Schools*. Available from: www.jubileecentre.ac.uk (accessed September 2015).

Arthur, J., Kristjánsson, K., Cooke, S., Brown, E. and Carr, D. (2015) *The Good Teacher: Understanding virtues in practice*. Birmingham: University of Birmingham. Available from: www.jubileecentre.ac.uk/userfiles/jubileecentre/pdf/Research%20Reports/The_Good_Teacher_Understanding_Virtues_in_Practice.pdf (accessed September 2015).

Association of Teachers and Lecturers (ATL) (2015) *Conference report*. 30 March – 1 April 2015. London: ATL. Available from: https://www.atl.org.uk/Images/ATL_Executive_Report_2015.pdf (accessed 20 December 2015).

Ball, S. J. (2001) Better read: Theorizing the teacher. In Dillon, J. and Maguire, M. (eds) *Becoming a Teacher: Issues in secondary education*. Buckingham: Open University Press. pp.10-21.

Ball, S. J. (2003). The teacher's soul and the terrors of performativity. *Journal of Education Policy*, 18 (2): 215–28.

Ball, S. J. (2006) *The Selected Works of Stephen J. Ball.* London: Routledge.

Beijaard, D., Meijer, P. and Verloop, N. (2003) Reconsidering research on teachers' professional identity. *Teaching and Teacher Education*, 20: 107–28.

Berkowitz, M. W. (1997) The complete moral person: anatomy formation. In Dubois, J. M. (ed.) *Moral Issues in Psychology: Personalist contributions to selected problems*. Lanham, MD: University Press of America.

Berkowitz, M. W. and Bier, M. C. (2005) *What Works in Character Education? A Research-driven Guide for Educators.* Washington, DC: Character Education Partnership.

Birdwell, J., Scott, R. and Reynolds, L. (2015) *Character Nation: A DEMOS report with the Jubilee Centre for Character and Virtues.* London: Demos.

Borba, M. (2002) *Building Moral Intelligence: The seven essential virtues that teach kids to do the right thing.* San Francisco, CA: Jossey Bass.

Bourdieu, P. (2000) *The Logic of Practice*. Cambridge: Polity Press.

Bronfenbrenner, U. (1979) *The Ecology of Human Development*. Cambridge, MA: Harvard University Press.

Carter, A. (2015) *Carter Review of Initial Teacher Training (ITT)*. Available from: https://www.gov.uk/government/uploads/system/uploads/attachment_data/file/399957/Carter_Review.pdf

Carr, D. (2007) Character in teaching. *British Journal of Educational Studies*, 55(4): 369–89.

Carr, D. (2016) Virtue ethics and education. In Snow, N. (ed.) *Oxford Handbook of Virtue*. Oxford: Oxford University Press.

Carrington, B. and Skelton, C. (2003) Re-thinking 'role models': Equal opportunities in teacher recruitment in England and Wales. *Journal of Education Policy*, 18 (3): 1–13.

Clarken, R. H. (2009) Moral intelligence in the school. Paper presented at the annual meeting of the Michigan Academy of Sciences, Arts and Letters, Wayne State University, Detroit, MI, March 20. Available from: http://files.eric.ed.gov/fulltext/ED508485.pdf (accessed 14 December 2015).

Coffey, A. (2001) *Sociology and Social Change Education and Social Change*. Maidenhead: Open University Press.

Cooper, K. and Olson, M. R. (1996) The multiple 'I's' of teacher identity. In Kompf, M., Bond, W. R., Dworet, D. and Boak, R. T. (eds) *Changing Research and Practice: Teachers' professionalism, identities and knowledge* London: Falmer Press. pp.78–89.

Department for Education (2011) *Teachers' Standards*. London: The Stationery Office.

Dermott, E. (2012) Troops to teachers: Solving the problem of working class masculinity in the classroom? *Critical Social Policy*, 32(2): 223–41.

Department for Education (2011) *Teachers' Standards*. London: DfE.

Department of Education (2013) *Teachers' Standards Guidance for school leaders, school staff and governing bodies*. London: Department of Education. Available from: www.gov.uk/government/uploads/system/uploads/attachment_data/file/301107/Teachers__Standards.pdf (accessed 20 December 2015).

Department for Education (2015) *Improving the Quality of Teaching and Leadership*. London: The Stationery Office.

Doherty, R. A. and McMahon, M. A. (2007) Politics, change and compromise: Restructuring the work of the Scottish teacher. *Educational Review*, 59 (3): 251–65.

Draper, J. and O'Brien, J. (2006) *Induction: Fostering career development at all stages*. Edinburgh: Dunedin Academic Press.

Elliot, J. (2004). Introduction, Making teachers more accountable: models, methods and processes. *Research Papers in Education,* 19 (1): 7–14.

Foster, T. and Newman, E. (2005) Just a knock back? Identity bruising on the route to becoming a male primary school teacher. *Teachers and Teaching*, 11 (4): 341–58.

Francis, B., Skelton, C. and Smulyan, L. (2006) *The Sage Handbook of Gender and Education*. London: Sage.

Hardy, I. (2008) The impact of policy upon practice: an Australian study of teachers' professional development. *Teacher Development*, 12 (2): 103–14.

Haydon, G. (1995) Thick or Thin? The cognitive content of moral education in a plural democracy. *Journal of Moral Education*, 24 (1): 53–64.

Hoyle, E. (1969) *The Role of the Teacher.* London: Routledge.

Jones, D. (2007) Millennium man: Constructing identities of male teachers in Early Years contexts. *Educational Review*, 59 (2): 179–94.

Jubilee Centre for Character and Virtues (2014) *A Framework for Character Education in School.* Birmingham: Jubilee Centre for Character and Virtues, University of Birmingham. Available from: http://jubileecentre.ac.uk/userfiles/jubileecentre/pdf/other-centre-papers/Framework.pdf (accessed August 2015).

Kohlberg, L. (1970) Stages of moral development as a basis for moral education. In Beck, C. and Sullivan, E. (eds) *Moral Education.* Toronto: University of Toronto Press.

Kohlberg, L. (1976) Moral stages and moralization: The cognitive developmental approach. In Lickona, T. (ed.) *Moral Development and Behavior: Theory, research and social issues.* New York : Holt, Rinehart and Winston.

Kunzman, R. (2015) Talking with students who already know the answer. In Hauver James, J. (ed.) *Religion in the Classroom, Dilemmas for Democratic Education.* London: Routledge.

Levin, B. (1998) An epidemic of education policy: what can we learn from each other? *Comparative Education*, 34 (2): 131–42.

Lickona, T. (2005) *Character Matters.* New York, NY: Touchstone.

Lyons, D. (2010) *So Mr… What Did you Do at School Today? A qualitative exploration of the professional lives of male primary school teachers in Australia.* London: Lambert Academic Publishing.

Marquese, M. (1995) Sport and stereotype: From role model to Muhammad Ali. *Race & Class,* 36 (4): 1–29.

McGrath, K. and Sinclair, M. (2013). More male primary-school teachers? Social benefits for boys and girls. *Gender and Education*, 25 (5): 531–47.

Millard, E. (2010) Responding to gender differences. In Arthur, J. and Cremin, T. (eds) *Learning to Teach in the Primary School* (2nd edn). London: Routledge.

Ofsted (2008) *Rising to the Challenge: A review of the Teach First Initial Teacher Training Programme.* London: HMSO.

Paterson, C., Tyler, C. and Lexmond, J. (2014) *Character and Resilience Manifesto.* London: All-Party Parliamentary Group on Social Mobility. Available from: http://www.centreforum.org/assets/pubs/character-and-resilience.pdf (accessed 12 October 2015).

Pike, M. A. (2011) Christian schooling for secular students. *Journal of Research in Christian Education*, 20 (2): 1–17.

Raths, L. E., Harmin, M. and Simon, S. B. (1966) *Values and Teaching.* New York: Wiley.

Reynolds, C. (1997) Cultural scripts for teachers: Identities and their relation to workplace landscapes. In Kompf, M., Bond, W. R., Dworet, D. and Boak, R. T. (eds) *Changing Research and Practice: Teachers' professionalism, identities and knowledge.* London: Falmer Press. (pp. 78–89).

Rhodes, C. and Greenway, C. (2010) Dramatis personae: Enactment and performance in primary school headship. *Management in Education*, 24 (4): 149–53.

Sanderse, W. (2012) The meaning of role modelling in moral and character education. *Journal of Moral Education*, 42, 1: 28–42.

School Standards and Framework Act (1998) Available from: http://www.educationengland.org.uk/documents/acts/1998-school-standards-framework-act.pdf (accessed 20 December 2015).

Sachs, J. (2001) Teacher professional identity: Competing discourses, competing outcomes. *Journal of Educational Policy,* 16 (2): 149–61.

Shaw, J. (2004) *Education, Gender and Anxiety.* London: Taylor and Francis.

Shore, C. and Wright, S. (1999) Audit culture and anthropology: Neo-liberalism in British Higher Education. *The Journal of the Royal Antropological Institute*, 5 (4): 557–75.

Smith, C. (2010) Research with children, young people and families. In Brotherton, G., Davies, H. and McGillivray, G. (eds) *Working with Children, Young People and Families*. London: Sage.

Skelton, C. (2007) Gender, policy and initial teacher education. *Gender and Education*, 19 (6): 677–90.

Sumsion, J. (2000) Negotiating otherness: A male early childhood educator's gender positioning. *International Journal of Early Years Education*, 8 (2): 129–40.

Thornton, M. and Bricheno, P. (2000) Primary teachers careers in England and Wales: The relationship between gender, role, position and promotion aspirations. *Pedagogy, Culture and Society*, 8 (2): 187–206.

Thornton, M. and Bricheno, P. (2006) *Missing Men in Education.* Stoke on Trent: Trentham Books.

Tomlinson, J. and Little, V. (2000) A code of the ethical principles underlying teaching as a professional activity. In Gardner, R. Cairns, R. and Lawton, D (eds) *Education for Values: Morals, Ethics, and Citizenship in Contemporary Teaching*. London: Kogan Page.

Training and Development Agency for Schools (2007) *Professional Standards for Teachers.* London: TDA.

Tucker, S. (1999) Making the link: Dual 'problematisation', discourse and work with young people. *Journal of Youth Studies*, 2 (3): 283–95.

Tucker, S. (2004) Youth working: Professional identities given, received or contested? In Roche, J., Tucker, S., Thomson, R. and Flynn, R (eds) *Youth in Society* (2nd edn). London: Sage.

Vescio, J. A., Crosswhite, J. J. and Wilde, K. (2004) The impact of gendered heroism on adolescent girls and their sport role models. Paper presented at the Pre-Olympic Congress, *International Congress on Sport Science, Sport Medicine and Physical Education*. Thessaloniki, August.

Wilson, J., Williams, N. and Sugarman, B. (1976) *Moral Education*. London: Penguin Books.

10 Building character through co-curricular programmes

In this chapter you will:

- find out how extra (or co-)curricular activities link to character education;
- gain a better understanding as to how coaching, facilitation and reflection strategies build character;
- read a description of how some well-known and less well known extra-curricular activities build character.

Introduction

Almost every primary school in the UK offers an array of different activities that their pupils are encouraged to take part in either before, during or after the school day – and sometimes during school holidays. Schools offer these activities for a number of reasons – perhaps because they connect to a passion or pastime of one of the teachers or that they are integrated into an after-school club. Whether the intention is implicitly or explicitly stated, another reason that schools run sports, music, dance, drama and a multitude of other activities is that they provide excellent vehicles for character education. This is why when a school is challenged to point to their character education provision very often they point to the extra-curricular activities they put on for their pupils.

The APPG for Social Mobility (Paterson et al., 2014) has called for extra-curricular activities to be a formal part of teachers' employment contracts as they are so beneficial for building character. Likewise, some schools have sought to elevate the status of these activities by calling them co-curricular as opposed to extra-curricular activities. The use of '*co-*' is a way of demonstrating that the activities are judged to be on a par, beneficially, with more academically focused activities.

Co-curricular activities help build character in pupils for the following reasons:

- They aspire primarily at character development, as opposed to, for example, ensuring that a student is meeting an academic attainment goal. The temptation in some teaching and learning is to go for a 'quicker fix' and focus purely on the academic outcomes rather than the character development opportunities in the teaching activity. When primary schools run extra-curricular activities they often have more time and space to focus on character development as well as less pressure to meet particular outcomes.

- They provide an excellent opportunity to introduce students to real life opportunities that 'test' their characters – through doing they learn about being. The activities often involve trying out new experiences. The students might succeed or fail at any particular activity, but importantly, learning about character takes place whatever the outcome. Learning through experience is vital to the development of practical wisdom.

- They are a chance to 'test' out different virtues in different environments. Virtues nurtured in classroom environments can be tested further in different settings. For example, courage can be tested by asking a student to speak in front of their peers in school, and further tested by speaking at a public engagement in the community. Likewise students might perhaps learn as much if not more from undertaking a service activity in the local community, than one run in school. It is for this reason that school trips, overnight events and outdoor activities provide a great basis for the building of character and cultivating practical wisdom.

The importance of character coaching and facilitation

Participation in extra-curricular activities alone is perhaps not sufficient to ensure primary school pupils develop character. The members of staff in charge of running the activities, as well as those supporting them, have important roles to play as character coaches, facilitators and role models. Staff running the activities should be mindful that the role should not be simply limited to ensuring that any activity runs smoothly and safely, but also that they should play the role of a character coach. As a coach the responsibility is to actively seek out opportunities before, during or after an activity to build the character of those participating. Extra-curricular activities provide a chance for teachers to develop different relationships with their pupils than they might in the classroom. Many teachers report that they see a very different side to their pupils when they take part in activities such as music, art, sport or during trips away.

Coaching for character can be done in a number of ways – all of them different from a more traditional teaching role. The advantage of extra-curricular activities is the context that teachers work in with pupils is different, allowing for a different type of relationship to form. The focus might be less on managing a class and more on developing strengths in individual pupils. The expectation of character coaching is not managing classroom performance but mentorship. Therefore, whereas a teacher might strive to pull their pupils towards a marked goal from the front, a coach would strive to push them towards this goal from a less dominant position. This involves:

- seeing the strengths and weaknesses of individual pupils – rather than the whole class's strengths and weaknesses;

- talking specifically to students individually (perhaps quietly on the side) rather than making more general comments on performance;

- spotting opportunities to coach for character whilst an activity is in flow;

- seeing the coach/pupil relationship as two-way – it is more about conversation than instruction;

- keeping character at the front of their mind and making specific reference to pupils' character during an activity, rather than simply concentrating on whether the activity was a success or not.

Character coaching: a language for character development

(adapted from the Primary Programme of Study developed by the Jubilee Centre for Character and Virtues and written by Geoff Smith, Kelhelland School)

The language coaches use is a powerful tool to develop and shape character and to help children be aware of and make progress in their moral development. Character coaching aims to replace the use of overused and non-specific phrases such as 'well done' or 'good' which do not give any specific indication of what was well done or good. Instead, if a pupil is praised for showing the virtue of determination in completing a piece of work and also given a chance to reflect on their experience of determination, then a link with an enduring character quality is established and any corresponding raising of self-esteem and self-respect will rest on a meaningful platform. Coaching involves asking very specific open questions to help others to understand more fully: our role when coaching is to ask, not to tell. In terms of character education, what matters most is that young people come to understand the presence and role of virtue in their lives. This arises from a level of self-awareness and understanding stemming from how we as teachers guide them to reflect on the events and stories of their lives. The main points of focus of these questions should be:

- noticing what is happening around us;

- noticing what we feel and what others feel: reading the information provided by emotion;

- noticing what we think and what others think: giving and taking reasons for action;

- reflecting on how our thoughts, speech and actions shape habits and affect who we are becoming.

Our daily interactions with pupils are likely to fall into three areas: meaningful praise, guidance, or correction. Meaningful praise involves identifying something specific that a child or group has done and helping them to reflect on how that is beneficial at the individual or group level. Shedding light on times when children use virtues can help them to recognise and understand the virtue and use it again. Guidance involves helping children to understand a virtue in a new way, or to see its application in their lives from a different angle. Correction involves noticing when a child says or does something which doesn't contribute to their own good or the overall good of the class or community. Rather than admonishing or telling off, correction is about helping the child to understand the impact of what they are doing and to see that there are virtues they can develop which may help them contribute to the good. Some people find the image of a cabinet maker bending and shaping a piece of wood helpful in envisaging correction. Of course, character coaching does not need to be done by teachers. Children can gather together in pairs or small groups to coach each other and enable learning from each other's experiences.

Here are some suggested examples of phrases that recognise and shape character.

Meaningful praise:

Example: When a pupil shows determination:

- Can you tell me what happened? What was it that helped you to keep going? Have you got any examples of other people doing the same thing as you?

When a pupil is friendly and considerate when welcoming new children:

- How did those children respond to you when you were friendly and considerate?
- How do you think it affected the rest of their day at our school?

Guidance:

Example: When a pupil is lacking in determination when trying something new or difficult:

- Think of a time when you have been determined and persevered. What did you feel or think then that can help you be determined with this?
- Think of people you know who have shown determination. What did they do or think?
- How can you use their experiences to help you?

Correction:

Example: When pupils are being inconsiderate by being noisy in the library:

- Have you noticed how your noise levels are different to everyone else's?
- What effect do you think this might be having?
- What do you need to change?

When a pupil is unkind to another:

- Did you notice what happened when you said X?

- What was the effect of your words?

- What would be a kind thing to do or say now?

Tools for reflection

Socrates said that 'the unexamined life is not worth living' – so a belief that personal reflection is part of character development is not new. As has been discussed, Aristotle believed that responsible action requires *phronesis* – the ability to make wise judgements on different courses of action. Encouraging pupils to reflect on what action they might take prior to an activity means they are more likely to hit the 'golden mean' – the mid-point between excess and deficiency of a virtue. Likewise, reflecting on an activity retrospectively allows pupils to make a critical assessment of what they did, what went well and what could have gone even better. The connection between personal reflection and personal learning is well documented in the literature (see, for example, Kolb's learning cycle (1984)). Encouraging pupils to reflect also helps to get beyond any sense that character education is indoctrinating or about obedience to a single point of view. Lockwood (2009) argues that reflection is a key ingredient in internalising personal values and taking ownership over them. Likewise, Baggini (2011) believes that personal reflection in moral education is a good response to those who say it might be indoctrinating as, in the process, pupils are being made to think for themselves and own the process of doing so.

A character coach can also introduce tools and approaches that will help the pupils reflect on their character development before, during and after any extra-curricular experience or series of experiences. Reflection helps ensure that these activities are successful vehicles for building character. The role of the teacher is to initiate opportunities for the pupils to reflect on their virtues before, during and after participation in a one-off or series of extra-curricular activities. Reflection strategies to enhance such learning might include: private or public prior reflection on what the pupils hope to gain from the activity; character coaching during the activity where the teacher directs questions that encourage the pupils to think about the virtues they are displaying; and reflection after that enables the pupils to think about what they have learnt about taking part and what they might do differently next time.

The activities initiated by the teacher might be more or less formal in nature. Examples of more formal reflection strategies include character logs, passports or journals where pupils record their character development journey in writing as they progress. Writing can involve pupils having to think deeply and give reasoned responses for their actions. Halberg (1987, p.289) says that such reflective writing can be 'person making' as it can change students' enduring attitudes, values, and sense of personal identity. The writing tools might be highly structured and involve pupils identifying at the outset particular character virtues they hope to develop through the experience and keep a record of progress towards achieving these goals as they advance through the activity. Informal reflection activities include more casual discussions between pupils and teachers during the activity, or peer to peer reflection times built into the activity programme. Many schools are also introducing strategies such as mindfulness and silent reflection to encourage pupils to think calmly about self and others. Mindfulness in particular is becoming increasingly popular in schools as a way to encourage pupils to think about who they are in the present. Reflections might be very short, say a minute or two at the start of each lesson, but regular and punctuate the school day to ensure pupils are constantly in touch with their character.

Building character through extra-curricular activities

In this section a number of extra-curricular activities run by primary schools are described. Within each description, the potential for character education is explored.

Sports clubs

Almost every primary school in the UK runs sports clubs – be they football, netball, cricket, rugby, gym, rounders or some other sport. The number of clubs run is a testament to the popularity of sport with 5–11 year olds, but also to their character building potential. Fundamentally, sport provides a controlled context for the development of character. Sport, or PE, is also a curriculum subject, and the National Curriculum for PE programmes of study for Key Stages 1 and 2 states: *'opportunities to compete in sport and other activities build character and help to embed values such as fairness and respect'*.

Most obviously sports (particularly team sports) are seen as a way to develop performance virtues such as self-discipline, teamwork, leadership, determination and communication. These are perhaps seen as fundamental to being successful teams and therefore winning. However, sports are also a great chance to build moral virtues such as humility, fair play and integrity. In many professional sports these are recognised as equally important as the performance virtues (as epitomised by the Olympic spirit) – and probably just as fiercely debated in the press. If a football player is deemed to have cheated it is as big a news story as that of another who scores a great goal. The moral virtues are part and parcel of sport. Therefore, it is important that they are given equal billing in sports coaching as performance virtues and the development of skills.

An important question to consider is does the very act of participation in a sports team build character, or does this have to be more carefully managed through facilitation by teachers and other staff? Are character virtues taught or caught in the playing fields? Most likely the ability to ensure these virtues are taught explicitly as well as caught implicitly is in the hands of the member of staff running the activity. It might be that getting better at a sport is achieved through practice, although most people would argue that the teaching of skills and techniques is just as important. Likewise, coaching is required for sports-based character education. A primary school sports coach recognises when pupils are cheating, not playing fair, or being arrogant and they should make an attempt to correct this. They might employ strong-handed methods to do this – some of them even punitive, such as removing players from a game. However, a better way is for coaches to spot potential acts of a lack of sportsmanship and pick these up with the pupils at the time and force them to take responsibility for their own character development. Coaches can challenge pupils to act differently the next time they are tempted to cheat or gloat when they win. This requires the staff member to be attentive, skilful at questioning and know what is required to get the best out of a pupil. Coaching involves reminding the young people what they are doing or learning in each moment; pointing out when they have shown perseverance in gym, telling a pupil they have shown great courage to lift their feet off the floor in the pool to begin to swim, or reminding pupils to shake the hand of a competitor at the end of a race that's been lost, to show respect. Another important aspect is of course how the staff (as well as any parents watching on) model these virtues themselves.

Environmental clubs

Environmental or eco-clubs are popular in schools – particularly with growing concern about sustainability and the environment. These clubs are a good chance to develop environmental virtues in pupils. Some of these clubs are connected to recognised national programmes like Eco-schools (an award programme that guides schools on their sustainable journey, providing a framework to help embed these principles into the heart of school life. Others set up their own clubs like St Bridget's Catholic Primary school in Birmingham, which runs a global gang consisting of about 20 pupils who have applied to join. The Global Gang looks at world cultures and global issues such as fair trade and acts to inform the whole parish community and lead parish events. Many other schools have Eco Warriors – where two pupils per class lead on sustainability issues, such as ensuring lights are off, recycling is done and litter is collected. Hursthouse (2007), amongst others, provides new interpretations of traditional virtues and applies these to how humans might best relate to nature. Important sustainability virtues for Hursthouse include prudence, practical wisdom, compassion, benevolence, unselfishness, honesty, patience and long-sightedness. These can be contrasted to vices that are often cited as the causes of unsustainability such as greed, self-indulgence, short-sightedness, cruelty, pride, and vanity.

A virtue ethical framework appears particularly promising when engaging young people in environmental issues. As sustainability is beset with complex problems and concerned with balancing conflicting needs – individual, social and environmental – these often result in virtues coming into conflict with each other. Phronesis is therefore an important virtue to foster in young people, as they are required to moderate complex problems. The cultivation and habituation of eco-virtues is also inherent in virtue ethics. Taking a virtue ethical stance on matters of the environment can be viewed as a positive, as developing virtues is seen as contributing to flourishing, rather than in terms of restraint or prohibition on actions.

Environmental clubs in primary schools could be structured around these virtues. Through practical activities the virtues of prudence, thrift and others can be explored. These might include pupils designing and developing recycling solutions or working out how best to make a little go a long way.

Forest Schools

The Forest School concept is an increasingly popular approach in primary schools to taking learning outside the classroom. The concept of Forest Schools started in Scandinavia and has been adopted by many schools in Britain. These schools have trained up members of their staff to deliver Forest School activities to pupils as young as five years old. The aim of running a Forest School is to create a learning community that all young people can thrive in. Within this community young people develop values, skills and attitudes that complement the core curriculum – but are also seen as equally important to it. The activity can be seen as a good form of character education as it encourages pupils to experience appropriate risk and challenge, undertake independent learning and self-development, develop positive relationships with themselves and other people as well as a strong, positive relationship to the natural world. The principles of Forest Schools that most closely relate to character education include: using a range of learner-centred processes to create a community for being, development and learning; promoting the holistic development of all those involved, fostering resilient, confident, independent and creative learners; offering learners the opportunity to take supported risks appropriate to the environment and to themselves. There are at least 25 Forest School companies in the UK, who train primary school teachers to be Forest School leaders. During these training events as well as in their portfolios, teachers are expected to consider the character qualities and strengths of the pupils experiencing the programme.

Debating clubs

Debating clubs might have been seen as traditionally the reserve of secondary and/ or independent schools. However, increasingly primary schools are seeing the character development potential of them. National programmes such as Debate Mate run teacher training as well as place university mentors to run after-school programmes. They do so because they see the character development opportunities in debating that contribute to social mobility. The organisation claims that their programmes *raise speaking and listening attainment as well as improve a range of high order thinking skills and non-cognitive abilities such as confidence, teamwork and leadership*' (http://debatemate.com/about-us/why-we-do-it/). Recent research from the University of Bedfordshire and the English-Speaking Union revealed that learning to debate can improve children's SATs results by between 6 and 19 per cent in all subjects (see www.esu.org/members-and-alumni/uk-branches/east/ouse-valley/misc/Primary-School-Research). The topics chosen for debate can also encourage students to discuss ethical dilemmas. Questions might include: should bullies be excluded from school?; should school children give some of their pocket money to charity?; and can anyone be a teacher? – all will get pupils to consider questions of character.

School trips

School trips are common to most schools – whether they be for the day, overnight or longer. These trips are often greeted with great enthusiasm by the pupils as they are seen as fun. They offer another vehicle for character education. Some trips will develop character through the choice of activity – for example a visit to the Holocaust museum will force pupils to consider what it means to be a 'good' and 'bad' person. Other trips will build character through the type of activities that the pupils engage in. For example a popular trip is an adventure holiday, perhaps run alongside an organisation like PGL or YHA. The activities themselves will build aspects of character such as team-working, resilience, leadership. However, a common by-product of the trip is an enhanced bond between pupils and their peers, and as importantly between pupils and their teachers. By working with pupils in a different context, teachers are able to capitalise on the relationships developed on these trips for the rest of the year. They are also able to 'coach' pupils in a different environment and context and many teachers say that they spot different character traits and qualities of their pupils while on school trips than they do in the classroom. Much of the character development that takes place on these trips is translated to the classroom.

School councils

School councils are very popular in primary schools. These normally consist of a group of pupils who are elected to represent the views of all the other pupils and to improve their school. If they are run effectively they are not only a good way to ensure that pupils' voices are fed into the management and organisation of the school – but they can also have the double benefit of developing the character of those on the council. They can be a great way to introduce students to civic virtues and a desire to serve others. To be a member of a school council the pupil must be willing to give up their time and undertake activities that will help their peers and the school community as a whole. Activities that the council undertakes – such as special projects, and putting on events – can develop character qualities, such as leadership, teamwork and creativity. As the council is expected to be a force for good in the school, the pupils need to demonstrate qualities such as resilience to get their voices heard, and tolerance and respect for everyone in the school community – not just the most popular pupils. Being a member of a school council is therefore a good microcosm in which to learn about social justice and fairness.

Chapter summary

In this chapter the links between character education and extra-curricular activities have been explored. Many enlightened schools have seen the potential for extra-curricular activities to build character, and have given them similar or equal status to the academic curriculum. The chapter explained the different relationship that teachers might adopt with their pupils whilst running such activities. It is suggested that considering yourself a character coach as opposed to a teacher would help ensure that you focus on the character-building potential of the activities as much as ensuring that they run smoothly and safely. A number of popular extra-curricular activities were discussed in the chapter – including sports clubs, environmental clubs, debating clubs, Forest Schools and school trips. Each was shown to be an excellent vehicle to develop different types of character virtues – mostly moral and performance.

Further reading

Arthur, J. and Harrison, T. (2013) *Schools of Character.* Birmingham: University of Birmingham, Jubilee Centre for Character and Virtues. Available from: http://www. jubileecentre.ac.uk/userfiles/jubileecentre/pdf/character-education/SchoolsOfCharacterPDF.pdf

In this publication seven schools are studied as they showcase a variety of approaches to character education. The schools are all different: some are primary, some secondary; some are independent, some are state-run, and one is a free school. However, they all have one thing in common – a belief that the development of their students' character comes before everything else. They believe that if good character is successfully nurtured in their students then everything else important, including good exam results, good job prospects and good behaviour, will follow. Whilst all of them make character education central to their vision and aims, they do so in different ways. In all the schools the importance of extra-curricular activities for character education is highlighted.

Seider, S. (2012) *Character Compass: How powerful school culture can point students towards success.* Cambridge, MA: Harvard Education Press.

This book offers portraits of three high-performing urban schools in Boston, Massachusetts, that have made character development central to their mission of supporting student success, yet define character in three very different ways. One school focuses on students' moral character development, another emphasises civic character development, and the third prioritises performance character development. Drawing on surveys, interviews, field notes and student achievement data, *Character Compass* highlights the unique effects of these distinct approaches to character development as well as the implications for parents, educators, and policymakers committed to fostering powerful school culture in their own school communities.

References

Baggini, J. (2011) Does Character Exist?. In Lexman, J. and Grist, M. (eds) *The Character Inquiry*. London: DEMOS. pp. 35–42.

Halberg, F. (1987) Journal writing as person making. In Fulwiler, T. (ed.) *The Journal Book*. Portsmouth, NH: Heinemann.

Hursthouse, R. (2007) Environmental virtue ethics. In Walker, R. L. and Ivanhoe, P. J. (eds) *Working Virtue: Virtue ethics and contemporary moral problems*. Oxford: Clarendon Press. pp.155–71.

Kolb, D. A. (1984) *Experiential Learning: Experience as a source of learning and development*. Englewood Cliffs, NJ: Prentice Hall.

Lockwood, A. (2009) *The Case for Character Education: A developmental approach*. New York: Teachers College Press.

Paterson, C., Tyler, C. and Lexmond, J. (2014) *Character and Resilience Manifesto*. The All-party Parliamentary Group on Social Mobility. www.centreforum.org/assets/pubs/character-and-resilience.pdf (accessed 12 October 2015).

11 Working with parents and the community

In this chapter you will:

- discover a range of sources that schools can draw on to support their character education provision;
- gain an overview of some of the resources in the voluntary sector that help schools deliver character education;
- discover the link between civic engagement and character education;
- read some hints and tips on how best to develop a partnership with parents on character education.

Introduction

Schools don't exist and function in a vacuum but occupy a unique position at the heart of their communities. The rhetoric goes that schools should 'serve' their communities, but the onus should be on organisations and individuals in the community also to 'serve' their local schools – they need to be mutually supportive of each other. Good schools spend time reflecting on the question, what sort of young people do we need to educate in order for the local community to flourish? The answer to this question is normally that we need young people with particular knowledge or skills (although essentially for employment), but we also need young people with good character who can play a positive full role as a member of the community. If a school can help to educate enough young people with good character, who want to be active and positive citizens, then this can truly transform a community within a generation.

It is also clear that those in a school's local community are interested in character. Ask a resident about their local school and they are more likely to make a comment about the character of the pupils than perhaps the schools' academic results. Parents might have a greater focus on exam results, but residents are more likely to notice how the pupils behave when they leave school – if they are noisy, drop litter, or are rude on the bus home. Schools therefore have a responsibility to help develop young people that their communities will be proud of. This should be an aspiration for any vision of character education. It is also something for which the school should turn to their community for support. Schools don't need to undertake the crucial job of developing the character of their pupils unaided, and should draw on the collective social capital around them. Layard and Dunn (2009, p.85) argue that it is essential that schools create and sustain links with their communities in order to develop values-based societies. After all, the role of a school is ultimately to prepare young people for life and work in the wider world. Most employers are more interested in employing someone with a good character than someone with a poor character and lots of qualifications.

The local community can be a great resource for schools. Most schools carry out the business of teaching and learning within the school gates, but they should look outside the school gates for support in carrying out their other very important role of helping to develop citizens with character. After all, schools are ultimately preparing students to be active and responsible citizens within these communities. Schools should encourage and support their students to take part in activities beyond the classroom, as such activities can have very positive benefits on the development of a young person's character. These types of educational activity are commonly referred to as experimental, or service or community-based learning.

> As Arthur (2003, p.143) comments, '{t}he aim of experimental learning in the community is not only to enhance critical reflection but to enhance personal development through opportunities to practice social and moral responsibility'. *He goes on to talk about how this type of learning both shapes and tests a young person's character. Students who take part in activities in their communities have both the opportunity to develop civic participation, but also develop their values. There are countless opportunities for schools to enable their students to take part in community-based activities which will in turn help them to develop and build their characters. Classic examples of such activities are undertaking an active citizenship project, volunteering or taking part in fundraising activities. These types of activities are regularly undertaken by students and it is important that schools and teachers recognise both the benefits they bring to the individual student as well as any benefits they bring to the community. The* Its Who You Are *report states that* 'activities such as residential trips, The Duke of Edinburgh scheme and students organising their own clubs, societies and discussion groups are instrumental in developing character, values and virtues' *(Arthur et al., 2006, p.12)*
>
> *(Arthur ed., 2010)*

The voluntary sector

The voluntary sector is a great source for schools seeking to extend and bring innovation to their character education provision. Developing partnerships with local, national or international voluntary sector organisations brings many benefits. These are explored in the following sections.

Substantial expertise in character education

Many youth work organisations specialise in running programmes for young people that develop their character. In a survey of 23 of the largest youth social action providers in the UK (working with 1 million young people a year between them) 57 per cent said that developing character was their primary aim (Arthur et al., 2015). The voluntary sector is full of individuals who not only have a great deal of expertise, but are also very passionate about building character in young people.

Resources

Although charities are subject to budget restrictions, often in a much greater way than are schools, many have funding specifically to run character education activities. Resources might include packs on specialist topics, such as on sustainable development or charity fundraising. Many organisations have examples of projects, and models of how best to run them, already established. Using an 'off the shelf' package could save a busy teacher a great deal of time. In some cases charities are funded to work directly with schools on activities that build character – such as mentoring programmes. Some also have specialist education departments whose main remit is to develop teaching and learning programmes for younger people.

Links to volunteers

Using volunteers to run character education programmes can be a win/win situation. Volunteers can help out with activities that require an extra pair of hands, but also the volunteers themselves can be great character role models for pupils. As voluntary sector organisations work with volunteers all the time, so they are a good way to access them. For example, ReachOut is an organisation that specifically recruits university students to run character education mentoring programmes; likewise Lauriston Lights recruits students to run character education holiday clubs. Managing volunteers can actually be another job for a teacher, so maybe it is better to access volunteers through voluntary sector organisations who already have systems in place to undertake this management role. The organisations will have expertise at recruiting volunteers, to check they are suitable as well as making sure they have all the relevant and required polices in place to ensure that they are properly managed.

Recruiting younger volunteers also brings benefits from what is sometimes called 'near peer'. It gives pupils a chance to spend time with other younger people who are closer than most teachers to being their peers, but who are slightly more confident and experienced. Modelling by near-peers is an effective method of getting young people to relate to positive behaviours and qualities. They also bring pupils into contact with volunteers who have given their time to make a difference – which can be a powerful model to set.

Helping to make it real

The best character education is when it is real. It is not about learning the theory of good character in the classroom – it is about testing out your own character in genuine situations. Voluntary sector organisations can provide access to such experiences – by helping to set up and run activities in the community. Voluntary sector organisations are constantly dealing with 'current and real' issues in their area of expertise. They therefore have first-hand experience of these issues. This experience can be a great tool to cultivate enthusiasm in young people, which in turn is a prerequisite to encouraging learning.

Innovation and novelty

Staff at voluntary sector organisations may also approach the subject from a different perspective from a teacher. Whereas a teacher might be put off by the challenge of running any particular activity, a member of staff from a voluntary organisation might have more time and experience. They are also more likely to be able to think about how a particular character education activity might run innovatively – therefore offering pupils something different from what they might normally get at school.

Case Study: Developing character through service learning – Floreat Education

In April 2015, Floreat Education was awarded a grant from the Department for Education to develop an infant Character Programme for pupils in Reception to Year 2. The programme aims to develop:

- pupils' virtue literacy – their understanding and language of 18 selected virtues;
- pupils' virtue behaviour – opportunities to put the virtues into practice through a series of Service Learning Projects;
- teachers' skills in modelling and delivering the programme, through the creation of teacher training materials.

An important part of developing pupils' virtue behaviour takes place during their Service Learning Projects. Service Learning Projects (SLPs) are weekly and timetabled opportunities for pupils to make a sustained commitment to engaging and supporting the community. Service Learning is a popular US approach to community engagement and has recently been successfully adopted at English schools, including Wellington College in Berkshire. The pioneering work that Floreat Education is focused on is bringing the benefits of this community service to a younger audience of 4–7 year olds. In the Early Years, Floreat SLPs invite the local community – for example, parents and extended family – to the school to partake in 'get to know you' tea parties and gardening projects. As pupils progress through the school, the aspiration is to involve local community partners in setting up and running projects for the benefit of a broader community, with pupils playing an active and ongoing role in the world beyond the school walls.

Floreat Education's approach to implementing Service Learning Projects is founded on a set of principles which has character development at its heart. These principles are as follows:

1. Human flourishing requires the development of civic virtues, such as service to the community – local and further afield.

2. The very best education promotes democratic citizenship and pupils' belief in their own responsibility to act and make a positive difference.

3. Service is for the benefit of the whole community.

4. Genuine service does not require praise or reward – character is what you do when no-one is looking – though there will be many opportunities for pupils to celebrate collective achievements.

5. SLPs can foster additional character virtues such as empathy and perspective, and leadership and teamwork.

The structure of each SLP follows a similar pattern, which ensures that pupils engage deeply with the project and aims to minimise administration for teachers. In any one SLP, pupils follow four stages:

1. Prepare: Pupils investigate a cause or need within the community and plan the action they will take, considering what they need to do to get ready. Examples: *Finding out about a topic, writing invitations for guests and speakers, making shopping lists.*

2. Act: This is the part of the project when pupils actively participate in service. Examples: *A book or toy drive, gardening, hosting an event, visiting members of the community.*

3. Celebrate: Where appropriate, there may be call for a celebration of the community's achievement. The nature of the celebration will vary depending on the project undertaken.

   Example: *A school gardening project might culminate in an event where the garden is opened to parents or peers in other year groups. In some instances, the action itself might double up as a celebration.* Example: *pupils hosting a tea party for their parents would count as both action and celebration.*

4. Reflect: Opportunities for structured cognitive and affective reflection take place throughout the SLP.

   Cognitive:

   What knowledge and skills did we use from our lessons?

   What new knowledge and skills have been learnt?

   Affective:

   How did I feel about...?

   What most surprised me about...?

   Examples of reflection activities in Early Years: *class scrapbook, circle time, display, video diary, newsletter, assembly, performance.*

→

In Floreat Schools SLPs are delivered through weekly taught sessions. Thirty minute lessons are timetabled for Reception with some flexibility required to accommodate the action and celebration aspects of the SLP. Alongside timetabled lessons, a relevant visual stimulus – such as a scene from *Alice's Adventures in Wonderland* for a tea party SLP – is often shown to pupils in the morning to provide an opportunity for the teacher to extend pupils' learning. The typical duration of a Floreat SLP is six weeks, though projects which yield particularly rich links to the knowledge curriculum can last a full 12-week term, meaning that children in Reception undertake 4-6 SLPs in the academic year.

Youth Social Action

Many voluntary organisations run what is now commonly termed youth social action programmes. Youth Social Action Organisations (YSAOs) are youth charities focused on delivering a double benefit of working with young people. The double benefit can be defined as:

1. building the skills and character that young people need to flourish as individuals as well as for the common good.

2. supporting young people to strengthen and (where necessary) drive change in society.

As the *Statement on Youth Social Action and Character development* (Jubilee Centre, 2014) states, *'through a dedication to social action the character of young people and the communities they live in can be transformed'*. There is an intrinsic link between Youth Social Action and character education as schools that help young people to plan, participate in and reflect on social action opportunities are also helping them to build their character. For example, consider the following character strengths that have been identified by the Department for Education as central to character education. These can all be developed by schools supporting young people to take part in Youth Social Action opportunities (see Jubilee Centre/Step up to Serve, 2015).

- Perseverance, resilience and grit – sticking at a youth social action project even when the going gets tough and it would be easier to quit.

- Confidence and optimism – growing in self-belief by successfully realising a personal or group vision for youth social action.

- Motivation, drive and ambition – youth-led social action projects taken on by young people to positively change something that they are passionate about.

- Neighbourliness and community spirit – participation in real life social action projects that involve the local, national or global community.

- Tolerance and respect – working alongside different people on social action projects, learning about each other, understanding difference and building mutual trust.

- Honesty, integrity and dignity – active participation in youth social action that purposely builds community spirit, trust and bonds.

- Conscientiousness, curiosity and focus – having the vision and desire to make a difference and applying oneself consistently to realise it.

Youth Social Action also helps pupils develop the overarching or meta-virtue of practical wisdom, as real life action is an opportunity to develop the ability to know what to do and what not to do, for the right reasons, in a variety of situations and contexts.

Step up to Serve is an umbrella body that has been recently established to increase young people's participation in social action. Every year the organisation (supported by the Jubilee Centre) recognises 50 IWill Ambassadors – 10–20 year-olds who have demonstrated outstanding youth social action. In the publication that showcases and celebrates the achievements of these young people they reflect on the many character virtues they have demonstrated and developed during their social action journeys. Reading the publication it is clear that many young people feel they have gained as much from their social action as they have given.

Case Study: All Saints C of E Junior School

All Saints is a primary school with 470 students. The school has recently sought to relaunch youth social action in the school and is half way through implementing radical curriculum changes that are partially centred on bringing the community into the school and creating volunteering and social action opportunities across the school. The school has six core values that were inspired by the London Olympics but were chosen by pupils and teachers. These values permeate everything that the school does and are used for recognition of the character virtues that students have gained throughout the school and curriculum. They use Monday celebration assemblies to high-light students who have achieved one of the school values through the 'Steps to Awesomeness' programme.

The interest in social action and character education stemmed from the staff noticing that some pupils struggled to acknowledge the positive aspects of their lives but had also developed a sense of mate-rialistic entitlement for their contributions. Because of this the school leadership wanted to help the children to see that material wealth and reward are not the key to happiness.

The staff admit there were challenges setting up a values-based youth social action programme that was an entitlement for all pupils. One commented that 'the programme started off a little bit slowly' as some of the staff and children were not sure what it was all about. However, after a slow start 'everyone has got more involved and appreciates where it's coming from. It has really picked up momentum with

→

children around the school now actively engaged with it and doing it for themselves'. The school staff have noticed a tension through rewarding positive examples of social action through a badge system – as they felt some pupils were doing it for extrinsic reasons. However, being in the programme is showing the pupils that when they do an act of service for somebody else it's good for them but also makes them feel good to help someone else.

Some examples of activities the pupils and local community take part in::

- The 'Guardian angels' project is where Year 6 pupils look after younger children in the playground, as well as listening to them read and other activities during the school day at lunchtimes and break times.

- Regular tea party events are held at the school for local community members to help tackle isolation and loneliness.

- Members of the congregation from All Saints Parish Church come in to help out in school in various ways, such as listening to the children read, playing the piano and helping out in various ways. They are also occasionally involved in the process of awarding badges.

- The school's 'Lunchtime Concert Club' sings in their local church choir as well as going into local retirement homes throughout the year.

Businesses and employers

Businesses are another potential source of support with character education. Most schools have either local, national or even global businesses on their doorsteps which can be drawn on in a number of ways. Businesses are often keen to support with character education as they understand their responsibility to help develop young people with the qualities and strengths required to be a good employees. Some will see character education as a core component of their Corporate Social Responsibility offer.

Businesses might be drawn on to support character education in one or more of the following ways:

- Role Models: Some individuals who have been successful in business can make good role models. They can be invited into schools to tell their stories. Stories of individuals who have had to strive through adversity, had a social mission and seen it through, and who understand the responsibilities that come with being in business all can make positive and inspiring messages.

- Mock interviews: A possibility is to get business people in to run interviews with Year 6 pupils. Although this may seem early in a child's life to be interviewed, it will encourage them to think about who they are and who they want to be. Interviews are largely about character, so they are a great way to introduce the importance of character to pupils.

- Resources: Running innovative character education initiatives can be a drain on resources. Businesses can be approached to support financially with extra costs or provide teams of volunteers for an afternoon to help support a particular activity.

Parents

The opening line of the *Framework for Character Education* (Jubilee Centre, 2013b) states that '*{d}eveloping children's characters is an obligation on us all, not least on parents*'. Although this book has primarily been about the role of primary schools and teachers to develop character in young people, it is important that parents are still considered the primary architects of their sons' and/or daughters' characters. Although young people spend a good proportion of their time in primary schools (around 650 hours in the classroom each year), parents have traditionally had the responsibility for bringing their children up well, with certain important attitudes and values. Although no parent would ever describe themselves as a character educator, this is effectively what they are doing. Parents, however, see the necessity for other people involved with their children's lives to take some of this responsibility. A poll carried out by Populus (Jubilee Centre, 2013a) found very strong support among parents for the idea that schools should be promoting character development alongside academic study. Eighty-seven per cent of parents in the study felt that schools should focus on character development and academic study, not simply academic study alone, and 84 per cent of parents felt that teachers should encourage good morals and values in students. Perhaps the most striking result is that 95 per cent of parents felt that it is possible for schools to teach a child values and shape their character in a positive sense through lessons and dedicated projects or exercises at school.

If schools are to be successful in their character education mission they must think about how best to work with parents. As the distinguished character educator Thomas Lickona observed '*schools that reach out to families and include them in character-building efforts greatly enhance their chances for success with students*' (Lickona, 1996). It stands to reason that such an alliance is crucial to the success of both effective schooling and parenting; for it is difficult to nurture virtues such as honesty, compassion and courage in schools, if these are neglected in the home – or vice versa.

Schools and parents forming partnerships on character sounds good in theory, but is of course much more difficult in practice. How can a successful partnership be formed initially and then maintained? Primary teachers meet parents on regular occasions – either after school or during more formal parents' evenings. Many of the discussions held at these meetings are probably about character, as much as attainment – but they are often unformulated and structured. Likewise, often primary schools award certificates and badges to pupils when they have been particularly helpful or overcome a challenge – however, these again are often spontaneous and unstructured. There is a practical challenge for teachers to go beyond functional communications home about, for example, behaviour or homework, and to develop a meaningful dialogue with parents built on long-term character development goals.

Some primary teachers might be concerned about taking more active and formal steps on active and genuine partnership with parents on character development as they are wary of the sensitive and potentially contentious territory they are entering. Below are three reasons why a teacher might be wary of forming partnerships with parents on character education:

- It is perhaps easier to talk to a parent about their son/daughter's progress in maths than to say that their son/daughter is involved with bullying.

- There may be a concern that teachers won't have the same character priorities as parents – and these might come into conflict. For example, a parent might be keen that their son/daughter wins at all costs on the sports field, whilst a teacher might feel it is their duty to encourage fair play and honesty in sport more than the result.

- There may be a possible tension or conflict between school and home values, making teachers nervous about promoting beliefs or perspectives to which parents might object.

Despite these concerns, schools are able to take steps that ensure serious practical cooperation between teachers and parents to help students acquire core character virtues that contribute to flourishing. A popular method is to include a section on character in communications between parents and teachers. This might involve some of the following:

- Developing character logs where pupils record activities (undertaken in and out of school) they have participated in that they feel they have learnt from and which have built their character. These logs are looked at and commented in by parents and teachers. They might contain an agreed set of character virtues that the pupil is keen to develop. The logs are a place where observations on the progress can be reported.

- Including a special section on character in end of year (or termly) reports to sit alongside statements about progress on different subjects. If nothing else, this section demonstrates that the school believes character development to be important and integral to teaching and learning.

- Writing a letter home to parents solely on the character development of their son/daughter at school. In the letter invite parents' comments and observations.

- As part of parents' meetings discuss with parents particular character targets for the pupils – so that they are mutually agreed. It might be that one term the target is for the pupil to show more resilience, or humility or patience.

An early step for a primary school seeking to bolster its character education provision would be to work with a group of parents to come up with creative and practical steps that successfully forge partnerships between parents and teachers on the very important business of character education. This might be a select group of parent governors or a facilitated session with the Parent and Teacher Association.

Case study: Knightly Virtues pupil journals

The Knightly Virtues Programme, developed by the Jubilee Centre for Character and Virtues, aims to develop character in pupils through reading and reflecting on great stories from the past – including *Don Quixote* and *The Merchant of Venice*. The aim of the programme is for pupils to think about the virtues displayed by the heroes and heroines in the stories and then reflect on how they might demonstrate similar virtues in their own lives – both in and out of school. Central to the success of the programme was a pupil journal where students recorded their thoughts and reflections on the stories and also related them to their own lives.

The architects of the programme thought that it was important that parents were invited to share or contribute to the learning experiences of their children. The journals provided an opportunity to do so. The pupils were encouraged by their teachers to take their journals home so that parents could read the stories with their sons/daughters as well as to take an active role in the completion of some of the activities and exercises. Parents were also asked to offer some comment in the journal – at a mid-point as well as at the conclusion of the programme. Analysis of these entries showed that the majority of parents were pleased that their sons and daughters were reading stories and welcomed the opportunity to (re)discover these stories alongside their children. The comments also suggested that the programme was the basis for stimulating rich conversations at home (as well as in school) about the character virtues, both in the stories themselves as well as in the lives of the children. During an evaluation of the programme it was also clear that the pupils themselves were touched by such parental approval and enthusiasm for the programme and the issues it explored.

The Knightly Virtues programme demonstrates the potential that well thought out and structured programmes have to encourage cooperation and partnership between teachers and parents on character education.

Chapter summary

There is a well-known African proverb that says that it takes a whole village to raise a child. This chapter has demonstrated how schools must work with parents and those in their local communities to build good character. It has shown how schools can draw on the wealth of resources and expertise in their community to support them in the important business of helping their pupils develop good character. Organisations in the voluntary sector often share a school's aim to develop character and can be great partners. Schools can provide access to pupils, whist voluntary organisations can provide access to resources, expertise and volunteers. Working with the voluntary sector also helps make an activity more real – embedded as part of the community. Although forming a successful partnership with

➤

parents on character education presents challenges for teachers, the chapter suggested some practical strategies that would help ensure that lines of communication over character education could be opened up and sustained to the benefit of pupils.

Further reading

Jubilee Centre (2104) *Statement on Character and Youth Social Action*. Available from: www. jubileecentre.ac.uk/userfiles/jubileecentre/pdf/StatementSocialAction.pdf

A short statement developed by an influential group of experts on how youth social action develops character virtues in young people.

Sercombe, H. (2010) *Youth Work Ethics*. London: Sage.

This books looks at what it means to practice youth work ethically. Although it is primarily aimed at youth work practitioners, many of the lessons and examples could also relate to schools offering civic engagement opportunities to their pupils. The book covers both ethical theory and practice – and looks at many topics that relate to the field such as managing dual relationships and working across cultures.

References

Arthur, J, Deakin-Crick, R, Samuel, E, Wilson, K. McGettrick, B. (2006) *Character Education: The formation of virtues and dispositions in 16–19 year olds*. Canterbury: Canterbury Christ Church University.

Arthur, J. (2003) *Education with Character: The moral economy of schooling*. London: RoutledgeFalmer.

Arthur, J. ed. (2010) *Citizens of Character: New directions in character and values education*, Exeter: Imprint Academic.

Arthur, J., Harrison, T. and Taylor, E. (2015) *Building Character – Through Youth Social Action*. Birmingham: University of Birmingham. Available from: http://www.jubileecentre. ac.uk/1574/projects/previous-work/character-and-service (accessed 13 January 2016).

Jubilee Centre (2013a) *Jubilee Centre Parents' Survey*. Birmingham: Jubilee Centre for Character and Virtues, University of Birmingham. Available from: http://jubileecentre.ac.uk/userfiles/ jubileecentre/pdf/character-education/ Populus%20Parents%20Study%20-%20short.pdf (accessed 1 December 2014).

Jubilee Centre (2013b) Framework for Character Education. Birmingham, University of Birmingham. http://jubileecentre.ac.uk/userfiles/jubileecentre/pdf/other-centre-papers/ Framework..pdf (accessed 8 December 2015).

Jubilee Centre (2014) Statement on Youth Social Action and Character Development. Birmingham: University of Birmingham. Accessed from: www.jubileecentre.ac.uk/userfiles/jubileecentre/pdf/StatementSocialAction.pdf (accessed 8 December 2015).

Jubilee Centre/Step up to Serve (2015) *Transforming Young People and Communities: Inspiring ideas from schools and colleges developing character through youth social action.* Birmingham: University of Birmingham. Available from: www.iwill.org.uk/resources/research/

Layard, R. and Dunn, J. (2009) *A Good Childhood: Searching for values in a competitive age.* London: Penguin.

Lickona, T. (1996) Eleven principles of effective character education. *Journal of Moral Education*, 25 (1): 93–100.

Part 4

Supporting Materials

This section contains some supporting materials that will help teachers and other educators implement character education in their school. Appendix 1 provides an audit of the book mapped against the Association of Character Education (ACE) principles. *The Framework for Character Education*, developed by the Jubilee Centre and its partners, is also reproduced in full in Appendix 2. In addition, in Appendix 3, there are recommendations for teaching materials and programmes as well as other books, papers and reports on character education.

Appendix 1

How to become a School of Character – self audit

The Association of Character Education (ACE) has suggested there are nine principles that schools of character should aspire to.

The table below highlights where advice can be found in this book that will help primary schools to meet the nine principles.

To see more about ACE and the principles visit www.character-education.org.uk.

Principle	A school of character...	Advice for meeting this principle in this book
1	...is committed to developing moral, civic, performance and intellectual virtues in all that it does	Chapter 2 – background to the four types of virtue Chapter 2 – strategies for drawing up a core list of virtues
2	...has a stated vision for character education actively promoted throughout the school	Chapter 8 – developing a vision for character education
3	...provides all students with tangible opportunities to develop their character	Chapter 6 – taught course Chapter 7 – teaching character through and within the curriculum Chapter 10 – extra-curricular activities
4	...is intentional, proactive and comprehensive in cultivating character	Chapters 6 and 7 – character taught Chapters 8, 9 and 10 – character caught
5	...understands the intrinsic and extrinsic benefits of good character	Chapter 1 – why character matters Chapter 3 – theories of flourishing
6	...has school leaders who are demonstrably committed to character education	Chapter 9 – teachers of character Chapter 8 – responsibilities of school leaders
7	...has teachers who share the vision for character education in the school and who take character education to be core to their role	Chapter 8 – whole staff responsibilities for character education Chapter 9 – teachers of character
8	...engages families and community members in cultivating character	Chapter 11 – working in partnership with parents, businesses and the voluntary sector
9	...can evidence that it has an effective character education strategy that is shared and understood by staff and students	Chapter 3 – challenges of measuring character Chapter 7 – assessment ideas Chapter 9 – strategies for measuring interventions

Appendix 2

A framework for character education in the UK

The *Framework for Character Education* was developed by the Jubilee Centre www.jubileecentre. ac.uk in consultation with head teachers, parents, academics, employers and young people both in Britain and internationally. It calls for all schools to be explicit about how they develop the character virtues of their students and explains the important role teachers play in making and shaping the character of young people in order for it to be properly recognised by parents, policy makers and employees.

Introduction

Developing children's characters is an obligation on us all, not least on parents. Although parents are the primary educators of character, empirical research shows they want *all* adults who have contact with their children to contribute to such education, especially their children's teachers. The development of character is a process that requires the efforts of both the developing individual and the society and its schools. A society determined to enable its members to live well will treat character education as something to which every child has a right. Questions about the kinds of persons children will become, the contributions of good character to a flourishing life, and how to balance various virtues and values in this process are therefore salient concerns for all schools. Interest is now being shown in character across a variety of UK schools. The aim of this Framework is to provide a *rationale* and a *practical outlet* for that interest.

No one doubts that belonging to a school community is a deeply formative experience that helps make students the kinds of persons they become. In a wide sense, character education permeates all subjects, wider school activities and general school ethos; it cultivates the virtues of character associated with common morality and develops students' understanding and embrace of what is excellent in diverse spheres of human endeavour. Schools do and should aid students in knowing the good, loving the good and doing the good. Schools should enable students to become good persons and citizens, able to lead good lives, as well as being 'successful' persons. Schooling is concerned centrally with the formation of character and benefits from an intentional and planned approach to character development.

Human flourishing is the widely accepted goal of life. To flourish is not only to be happy, but to fulfil one's potential. Flourishing is the aim of character education, which is critical to its achievement. *Human flourishing* requires *moral*, *intellectual* and *civic* virtues, *excellences* specific to diverse domains of practice or human endeavour, and generic virtues of *self-management* (known as *enabling* and *performance* virtues). All are necessary to achieve the highest potential in life.

Character education is about the acquisition and strengthening of virtues: the traits that sustain a well-rounded life and a thriving society. Schools should aim to develop confident and compassionate students who are effective contributors to society, successful learners and responsible citizens. Students also need to grow in their understanding of what is good or valuable and their ability to protect and advance what is good. They need to develop a commitment to serving others, which is an essential manifestation of good character in action. Questions of character formation are inseparable from these educational goals and are fundamental to living well and living responsibly. Character development involves caring for and respecting others as well as caring for and respecting oneself.

Character education is no novelty. If we look at the history of schooling from ancient to modern times, the cultivation of character was typically given pride of place, with the exception of a few decades towards the end of the twentieth century, when this aim disappeared, for a variety of reasons, from curricula in many western democracies.

Contemporary character education is, however, better grounded academically than some of its predecessors, with firm support both from the currently dominant *virtue ethics* in moral philosophy and recent trends in social science, such as *positive psychology*, that have revived the concepts of character and virtue. Finally, a growing general public-policy consensus, across political parties and industry, suggests that the role of moral and civic character is pivotal in sustaining healthy economies and democracies.

What character education is

Character is a set of personal traits or dispositions that produce specific emotions, inform motivation and guide conduct. *Character education* is an umbrella term for all explicit and implicit educational activities that help young people develop positive personal strengths called *virtues*. Character education is more than just a subject. It has a place in the culture and functions of families, classrooms, schools and other institutions. Character education is about helping students grasp what is ethically important in situations and to act for the right reasons, such that they become more autonomous and reflective. Students need to decide the kind of person they wish to become and to learn to choose between alternatives. In this process, the ultimate aim of character education is the development of *good sense* or practical wisdom: the capacity to choose intelligently between alternatives. This capacity involves knowing how to choose the right course of action in difficult situations and it arises gradually out of the experience of making choices and growth of ethical insight.

What character education is not

Character education is *not* about moral indoctrination and mindless conditioning. The ultimate goal of all proper character education is to equip students with the intellectual tools to choose wisely of their own accord within the framework of a democratic society. Critical thinking is thus an ineluctable facet of a well-rounded character. Character and virtue are *not* essentially religious notions although they do clearly have a place in religious systems. Almost all current theories of virtue and character education happen to be couched in a post-religious language. Character and virtue are *not* paternalistic notions. If being 'paternalistic' means that character education goes against the wishes of students and their parents, empirical research shows the opposite. More generally speaking, the character of children cannot simply be put on hold at school until they reach the age where they have become wise enough to decide for themselves. Some form of character education will always take place in any school. The sensible question that can be asked about a school's character education strategy is not, therefore, whether such education does occur, but whether it is intentional, planned, organised and reflective, or assumed, unconscious, reactive and random. The emphasis on character and virtue is *not* conservative or individualist – all about 'fixing the kids'. The ultimate aim of character education is not only to make individuals better persons but to create the social and institutional conditions within which all human beings can flourish. Character education is *not* about promoting the moral ideals of a particular moral system. Rather, it aims at the promotion of a core set of universally acknowledged (cosmopolitan) virtues and values.

Key principles

- Character is educable and its progress can be measured holistically, not only through self-reports but also more objective research methods.

- Character is important: it contributes to human and societal flourishing.

- Character is largely caught through role-modelling and emotional contagion: school culture and ethos are therefore essential.

- Character should also be taught: direct teaching of character provides the rationale, language and tools to use in developing character elsewhere in and out of school.

- Character is the foundation for improved attainment, better behaviour and increased employability.

- Character should be developed in partnership with parents, employers and other community organisations.

- Character results in academic gains for students, such as higher grades.

- Character education is about fairness and each child has a right to character development.

- Character empowers students and is liberating.

- Character demonstrates a readiness to learn from others.

- Character promotes democratic citizenship.

What virtues constitute good character?

Individuals can respond well or less well to the challenges they face in everyday life, and the moral virtues are those character traits that enable human beings to respond appropriately to situations in any area of experience. These character traits enable people to live, cooperate and learn with others in a way that is peaceful, neighbourly and morally justifiable. Displaying moral and other virtues in admirable activity over the course of a life, and enjoying the inherent satisfaction that entails is what it means to live a flourishing life.

No definitive list of relevant areas of human experience and the respective virtues can be given, as the virtues will to a certain extent be relative to individual constitution, developmental stage and social circumstance. For example, temperance in eating will be different for an Olympic athlete and an office worker; what counts as virtuous behaviour for a teenager may not pass muster for a mature adult; and the virtues needed to survive in a war zone may not be the same as those in a peaceful rural community. There are also a great many virtues, each concerned with particular activities and potential spheres of human experience. It is, therefore, neither possible nor desirable to provide an exhaustive list of the moral virtues that should be promoted in all schools. Moreover, particular schools may want to decide to prioritise certain virtues over others in light of the school's history, ethos, location or specific student population. Nevertheless, a list of *prototypical* virtues – that will be recognised and embraced by representatives of all cultures and religions – can be suggested and drawn upon in character education. The list below contains examples of such virtues that have been foregrounded in some of the most influential philosophical and religious systems of morality – and that also resonate well with current efforts at character education in schools:

Virtue	Definition
Courage	Acting with bravery in fearful situations
Justice	Acting with fairness towards others by honouring rights and responsibilities
Honesty	Being truthful and sincere
Compassion	Exhibiting care and concern for others
Self-discipline	Acting well in the presence of tempting pleasures
Gratitude	Feeling and expressing thanks for benefits received
Humility/modesty	Estimating oneself within reasonable limits

Furthermore, every morally developing human being will need one extra virtue which the ancient Greeks called *phronesis*, but can also be called 'good sense' – the overall quality of knowing what to want and what not to want when the demands of two or more virtues collide, and to integrate such demands into an acceptable course of action. Living with good sense entails: considered deliberation, well founded judgement and the vigorous enactment of decisions. It reveals itself in foresight, in being clear sighted and far sighted about the ways in which actions will lead to desired goals. The ability to learn from experience (and make mistakes) is at the centre of it. To live with good sense is to be open-minded, to recognise the true variety of things and situations to be experienced. To live without 'good sense' is to live thoughtlessly and indecisively. 'Bad sense' shows itself in irresoluteness, or remissions in carrying out decisions and in negligence and blindness to our circumstances. To live without 'good sense' is to be narrow-minded and close-minded; it can reveal itself in an attitude of being 'cock-sure' – a 'know-it-all' approach that resists reality. 'Good sense' cannot be confused with 'cunning'; 'cunning' reveals itself in non-moral straining for any self-chosen good. 'Good sense' forms part of all the other virtues; indeed it constitutes the overarching *meta-virtue* necessary for good character. It requires a well-rounded assessment of situations, thinking through and looking ahead to potential actions and consequences.

Virtues are empowering and are the key to fulfilling an individual's potential. Because of the foundational role of the virtues in human flourishing, schools have a responsibility to cultivate the virtues, define and list those they want to prioritise and integrate them into all teaching and learning in and out of school. Students therefore need to learn their meanings and identify appropriate practices in which to apply them in their lives, *respecting themselves* (as persons of character) and rendering *service* to others.

In addition to the moral virtues, all human beings need personal traits that enable them to manage their lives effectively. These traits are sometimes called *performance virtues* and *enabling virtues*, to distinguish them from the specifically moral ones. In contemporary school policy discourse, they are commonly referred to as 'soft skills'. One of the most significant of those is *resilience* or grit – the ability to bounce back from negative experiences. Others include determination, confidence, creativity and teamwork. All good programmes of character education will include the cultivation of performance virtues, but they will also explain to students that those virtues derive their ultimate value from serving morally acceptable ends, in particular from being enablers and vehicles of the moral virtues.

The goals of character education

It is common for a school to outline the goals of education in its mission statement, and a school that seeks to strengthen the character of its students should reaffirm its commitment to doing so in its mission statement.

Each school needs to describe the kinds of future citizens it wants to help develop and then outline the philosophy that underlies its approach. The philosophy and approach should involve clear ethical expectations of students and teachers, and modelling by teachers to guide the building of individual virtues in students. Schools should provide opportunities for students to not just think and do, but also understand what it means to be and become a mature, reflective person. They should help prepare students for the tests of life, rather than simply a life of tests.

School ethos based on character

The research evidence is clear: schools that are values-driven have high expectations and demonstrate academic success. They are committed and determined to develop the character of their students through the articulation, demonstration and commitment to core ethical virtues. Because the ethos of a school is the expression of the collective character of everyone, it is important for every member of a school community to have some basic understanding of what character is. Students and teachers therefore need to learn not only the names of character virtues, but display them in the school's thinking, attitudes and actions. Character virtues should be reinforced everywhere: on the playing fields, in classrooms, corridors, interactions between teachers and students, in assemblies, posters, head teacher messages and communications, staff training, and in relations with parents. They are critical in extra-curricular activities and should translate into positive feelings and behaviour. The process of being educated in virtue is not only one of acquiring ideas. It is about belonging and living within a community – for schools are, together with the family, one of the principal means by which students grow in virtue.

Teachers as character educators

Character education builds on what already happens in schools and most teachers see character cultivation as a core part of their role. Considerations of character, of the kind of person students hope to become, should be at the heart of teaching and education. The virtues acquired through experience by students are initially under the guidance of parents and teachers who serve as role models and moral exemplars.

In order to be a good teacher, one needs to be or become a certain *kind of person*: a person of good character who also exemplifies commitment to the value of what she teaches. The character and integrity of the teacher is more fundamental than personality or personal style in class, and it is no less important than mastery of subject content and techniques of instruction. Teaching a subject with integrity concerns more than helping students to acquire specific bits of knowledge and skills.

Good teaching is underpinned by an ethos and language that enables a public discussion of character within the school community so that good character permeates all subject teaching and learning. It also models commitment to the forms of excellence or goodness inherent in the subject matter: the qualities of craftsmanship, artistry, careful reasoning and investigations, beauty and power of language, and deep understanding made possible by the disciplines. Such commitment is important if students are to learn the value of what is taught and learn to do work that is good and personally meaningful.

Although a clear picture is emerging of the inescapability of character education, teachers often complain that they suffer from moral ambivalence and lack of self-confidence in their (inescapable) professional position as role models and character educators. Repeated empirical studies show that teachers find it difficult to address ethical issues in the classroom. Although many teachers possess a strong interest in moral issues, they are not always adequately trained to critically reflect upon and convey moral views to their students in a sophisticated way. Unfortunately, the recent surge in interest in character education has so far failed to make an impact on teacher education and training. Indeed, contemporary policy discourse, with its amoral, instrumentalist, competence-driven vocabulary, often seems to shy away from perspectives that embrace normative visions of persons in the context of their whole lives. The lack of teacher education programmes with a coherent approach to character education is most likely the result of more dominant principles of grade attainment and classroom management. This seems a lost opportunity, however, given the commonly expressed desire among trainee teachers to make a moral difference. It is fitting to end this Framework document with a call for increased attention to moral issues, in general, and character-educational issues, in particular, in teacher education and training.

References

Annas, J. (2011) *Intelligent Virtue*. Oxford: Oxford University Press.

Arthur, J. and D. Carr (2013) Character in learning for life: a virtue-ethical rationale for recent research on moral and values education. *Journal of Beliefs & Values: Studies in Religion & Education*, 34 (1): 26–35.

Arthur, J. A. (2010) *Citizens of Character*. Exeter: Imprint Academic.

Berkowitz, M. W. and Bier, M. C. (2004) Research-based character education. *The ANNALS of the American Academy of Political and Social Science*, 591 (1): 72–85.

Carr, D. (1991) *Educating the Virtues: Essay on the philosophical psychology of moral development and education.* London: Routledge.

Curren, R. (2010) Aristotle's educational politics and the Aristotelian renaissance in philosophy of education. *Oxford Review of Education*, 36 (5): 543–59.

Damon, W. (1988). *The Moral Child*. New York: The Free Press.

Durlak, J. A., Weissberg, R. P., Dymnicki, A. B., Taylor, R. D. and Schellinger, K. B. (2011) The impact of enhancing students' social and emotional learning: a meta-analysis of school-based universal interventions. *Child Development*, 82 (1): 405–32.

Kristjánsson, K. (2013) Ten myths about character, virtue and virtue education – and three well-founded misgivings. *British Journal of Educational Studies* (iFirst). Available from: http://www.tandfonline.com/doi/abs/10.1080/00071005.2013.778386#.UcQex9i658E (accessed 15 December 2015).

Lickona, T. (1991) *Educating for Character: How our schools can teach respect and responsibility*. New York: Bantam Books.

Nucci, L. P., Narváez, D. and Krettenauer, T. (eds) (2014) *Handbook of Moral and Character Education* (2nd edn). New York and London: Routledge.

Ryan, K. and Bohlin, K. (1999) *Building Character in Schools*. San Francisco, CA: Jossey-Bass.

Sanderse, W. (2012) *Character Education: A neo-Aristotelian approach to the philosophy, psychology and education of virtue*. Delft: Eburon Academic Publishers.

Sanger, M. N. and Osguthorpe, R. O. (2013) *The Moral Work of Teaching and Teacher Education*. New York: Teachers College Press.

Seider, S. (2012) *Character Compass: How powerful school culture can point students towards success.* Cambridge, MA: Harvard Education Press.

Sockett, H. and LePage, P. (2002) The missing language of the classroom. *Teaching and Teacher Education*, 18 (2): 159–71.

Appendix 3

Character education teaching resources

Below is a list of useful books, web based materials and other resources that will help primary practitioners explore the theory and practice of character education.

Character education teaching resources

Programme of Study – Primary

www.jubileecentre.ac.uk/1598/programmes-of-study/primary-resources www.jubileecentre.ac.uk/primaryprogramme

The programme of study provides a taught course in character education for reception to Year 6. The course is divided into three terms and separated into individual year groups. Each term's curriculum is divided into sequences of lessons which address particular virtues. The course allows flexibility to suit individual school/teacher approaches. Teachers' notes and accompanying PowerPoint presentations are also provided.

The Knightly Virtues Programme

http://www.jubileecentre.ac.uk/knightlyvirtuesresources

This educational programme seeks to provide nine to eleven year olds with the chance to creatively explore great stories of knights and heroes and the virtues to which they aspired. Drawing from timeless historical and literary narratives this programme is tailored towards encouraging pupils to enjoy reading about inspiring people, whilst helping them to consider their own virtues of character.

Framework for Character Education

http://www.jubileecentre.ac.uk/userfiles/jubileecentre/pdf/character-education/Framework%20 for%20Character%20Education.pdf

The Jubilee Centre for Character and Virtues' position on character education is set out in the *Framework for Character Education in Schools*. It calls for all schools to be explicit about how they develop the character virtues of their students and the important role teachers play in making and shaping the character of young people to be properly recognised by parents, policy makers and employees.

Statement on Character and Youth Social Action

www.jubileecentre.ac.uk/userfiles/jubileecentre/pdf/StatementSocialAction.pdf

A short statement developed by an influential group of experts on how youth social action develops character virtues in young people.

Schools of Character

http://www.jubileecentre.ac.uk/userfiles/jubileecentre/pdf/character-education/SchoolsOfCharacterPDF.pdf

This publication showcases seven schools (including two primary schools) that make character education a conscious part of their day-to-day practice through a variety of approaches. The case studies presented are designed to highlight the most pertinent features of character education in each of the schools and aim to provide both inspiration, as well as examples, for other schools seeking to develop their character education provision.

Teaching Character Through the Curriculum

http://www.jubileecentre.ac.uk/userfiles/jubileecentre/pdf/Teaching_Character_Through_The_Curriculum1.pdf

This publication, although primarily aimed at Secondary Schools, demonstrates how character might be taught through fourteen curriculum subjects. The links between character virtues and the pedagogical practices and content of each subject are also explored. For each subject, the virtues that might be considered most closely linked to it are emphasised and learning and teaching activities that develop character virtues in the classroom, across the whole school and in the community are suggested.

Thank You Letter Awards

www.jubileecentre.ac.uk/thankyouawards

This programme encourages primary and secondary pupils to write thank you letters to people who have inspired them. The writers of the best letters are recognised in a national celebration event.

Inspire/Aspire Awards

www.inspire-aspire.org.uk/

A programme run by Character Scotland for schools focused on developing values in young people through designing and developing a poster about their character.

Becoming Value-able

www.jubileecentre.ac.uk/userfiles/jubileecentre/pdf/previousresearch/Becoming_value-able.pdf

A set of nine teaching activities developed by Learning for Life that will enable young people to discover what values are and why they are important. The back of the booklet contains all the resources you need to carry out the activities.

Character Building

www.jubileecentre.ac.uk/userfiles/jubileecentre/pdf/previousresearch/Character_Building.pdf

Who are you? Who do you want to be? A teaching resource developed by Learning for Life that will enable young people to discover what character is needed to be successful in life as well as a successful member of society.

Books on character education

Arthur, J. (2003) *Education with Character: The moral economy of schooling*

An introduction to character education within the British context, exploring its meanings, understandings and rationale through the perspective of academic disciplines. The author examines character education from philosophical, religious, psychological, political, social and economic perspectives to offer a more detailed understanding of character education and what it can offer.

Morris, I. (2015) *Teaching Happiness and Wellbeing in Schools: Learning to ride elephants* (2nd edn). London: Bloomsbury.

There has recently been an explosion of interest in positive psychology and the teaching of well-being and 'happiness' in the PSHE world in schools and many teachers are looking for clear information on how to implement these potentially life-changing ideas in the classroom. This book provides an introduction to the theory of positive psychology and a practical guide on how to implement the theory in (primary and secondary) schools.

Kristjánsson, K. (2015) *Aristotelian character education*. London: Routledge.

This book provides a reconstruction of Aristotelian character education, shedding new light on what moral character really is, and how it can be highlighted, measured, nurtured and taught in current schooling. Arguing that many recent approaches to character education understand character in exclusively amoral, instrumentalist terms, the author proposes a coherent, plausible and up-to-date concept, retaining the overall structure of Aristotelian character education.

Carr, D. and Harrison, T. (2015) *Educating character through stories*. Exeter: Imprint Academic.

This book explores how character might be educated through stories. The book draws on the experience of developing and trialing the Knightly Virtues programme. The book presents the comprehensive philosophy behind the programme as well as practical lessons learned from implementing it in schools.

Annas, J. (2011) *Intelligent Virtue*. Oxford: Oxford University Press.

Intelligent Virtue presents a distinctive new account of virtue and happiness as central ethical ideas. Annas argues that exercising a virtue involves practical reasoning of a kind which can illuminatingly be compared to the kind of reasoning we find in someone exercising a practical skill. Rather than asking at the start how virtues relate to rules, principles, maximising, or a final end, we should look at the way in which the acquisition and exercise of virtue can be seen to be in many ways like the acquisition and exercise of more mundane activities, such as farming, building or playing the piano.

Arthur J. (2010) *Citizens of Character: New directions in character and values education*. Exeter: Imprint Academic.

This book presents a substantial body of empirical evidence about what parents, teachers and pupils are thinking and doing in the area of character education.

Brooks, D. (2015) *The Road to Character*. London: Allen Lane

A popular book by the *New York Times* journalist exploring the difference between résumé and eulogy virtues.

Lickona, T. (1992) *Educating for Character: How our schools can teach respect and responsibility*. New York: Bantam Books.

Lickona, a professor of education at the State University of New York addresses the controversial topic of 'values' education and its place in today's classrooms in this book. In a well-balanced presentation distilling his decades of experience, Lickona suggests practical approaches that have been developed by several programmes of moral education.

Seider, S. (2012) *Character Compass: How powerful school culture can point students towards success*. Cambridge, MA: Harvard Education Press.

In *Character Compass*, Seider offers portraits of three high-performing urban schools in Boston, Massachusetts, that have made character development central to their mission of supporting student success, yet define character in three very different ways. One school focuses on students' moral character development, another emphasises civic character development, and the third prioritises performance character development. Drawing on surveys, interviews, field notes, and student achievement data, *Character Compass* highlights the unique effects of these distinct approaches to character development as well as the implications for parents, educators, and policymakers committed to fostering powerful school culture in their own school communities.

Academic papers on character education

Arthur, J, Harrison, T. Davison, I. (2015) Levels of virtue literacy in Catholic, Church of England and non-faith schools in England: A research report. *International Studies in Catholic Education*, 7 (2): 178–200.

This article reports on an innovative empirical research project, using a quasi-experimental trial, in which 9–11-year-olds learned about character and virtues through the exploration of four classic stories. The overall aim of the programme was to enhance virtue literacy. Virtue literacy is defined as the knowledge, understanding and application of virtue language and is viewed as being integral to the development of character.

Arthur, J. (2005) The re-emergence of character education in British education policy. *British Journal of Educational Studies*, 53 (3): 239–54.

Character education is a specific approach to morals or values education, which is consistently linked with citizenship education. But how is it possible for a heterogeneous society that disagrees about basic values to reach a consensus on what constitutes character education? This article explores how character education has returned to the agenda of British education policy, having been largely neglected since the 1960s in response to unsatisfactory attempts at character education going back to the nineteenth century.

Kristjánsson, K. (2013) Ten myths about character, virtue and virtue education – and three well-founded misgivings. *British Journal of Educational Studies*, 61 (3): 269–87.

Initiatives to cultivate character and virtue in moral education at school continue to provoke sceptical responses. Most of those echo familiar misgivings about the notions of character, virtue and education in virtue – as unclear, redundant, old-fashioned, religious, paternalistic, anti-democratic, conservative, individualistic, relative and situation dependent. The paper exposes these misgivings as 'myths', while at the same time acknowledging three better-founded historical, methodological and practical concerns about the notions in question.

Walker, D., Roberts, M. and Kristjánsson, K. (2015) Towards a new era of education in theory and practice. *Educational Review,* 67 (1): 79–96.

The authors use a Bourdieuean framework of 'legitimating principles' and the 'symbolic capital' of dominant 'discursive themes' to explore (a) the genealogy and (b) the current state of the discourse on 'character education' (understood broadly as any approach to moral education that foregrounds the cultivation of moral character and moral virtue).

Lickona, T. (1996) Eleven principles of effective character education. *Journal of Moral Education*, 25 (1): 93–100.

This paper sets out 11 principles to guide schools as they plan their character education initiative.

Reports on character education

Character Education in UK Schools: Research Report

www.jubileecentre.ac.uk/characterandvirtueseducation

The research project described in this report represents one of the most extensive studies of character education ever undertaken, including over 10,000 students and 255 teachers in schools across England, Scotland, Northern Ireland and Wales. The research explored the formation of character in students in 68 UK schools and investigated how teachers view their role in developing good character and virtue in students.

The Good Teacher

www.jubileecentre.ac.uk/1554/projects/research-reports/the-good-teacher

The report sets out new research focusing on the virtues that good teachers might need and the role these virtues play in teaching. The research was conducted with 546 novice and experienced teachers.

Character Nation

http://www.demos.co.uk/publications/character-nation

This report by DEMOS provides a series of policy recommendations for governments to ensure that character development is embedded across the education system.

Character and Resilience Manifesto

http://www.centreforum.org/assets/pubs/character-and-resilience.pdf

A report from the All Party Parliamentary Group on Social Mobility on the importance of character and resilience for social mobility.

The Fruits of the Spirit: A Church of England Discussion Paper on Character Education

www.jubileecentre.ac.uk/userfiles/jubileecentre/pdf/Fruits_of_the_Spirit2015.pdf

In this paper the Church of England give their position on character education. The document explores the links between Christian world views and character, what character education might look like in a pluralist society, and how best to 'teach' character.

Transforming Young People and Communities

http://www.iwill.org.uk/resources/research

This publication developed by Step up to Serve and the Jubilee Centre for Character and Virtues highlights practical advice from 50 headteachers about how best to develop character through youth social action activities run by schools.

Index